What They're Saying About
WHO'S RUNNING YOUR CAREER?

"*Caela Farren is a master at inspiring, educating, and explaining the steps you need to take to achieve and surpass your career expectations in the Web of Work. Her words will lead you to new levels of career satisfaction and fulfillment.***"**

—Laurie Beth Jones
Author of *Jesus CEO, The Path,* and
Jesus in Blue Jeans

"*Take the fear out of career planning! This common-sense approach provides easy-to-understand guidance and shows how achieving mastery can be your great career advantage.***"**

—Kate Aiken Moody
Organizational Development Consultant
Liz Claiborne, Inc.

"*Valuable and timely information for everyone—if you're just out of college, in transition, or experienced, this is an essential career guide for our rapidly growing technological society.***"**

—Marian C. Diamond, Ph.D.
Professor, Department of Integrative Biology
University of California, Berkeley

"*You'll want to read this book cover to cover. The vital concepts and working examples will create confidence and structure as you move forward to career success.***"**

—Susan Tomlinson
Director, Career Action Centre
Cable and Wireless PLC

Who's Running Your Career?

Caela Farren, Ph.D.

Who's Running Your Career?

Caela Farren, Ph.D.

Bard Press

AUSTIN ★ ATLANTA

Who's Running Your Career?
Creating Stable Work in Unstable Times

Printed in the United States of America

Permission to reproduce or transmit in any form or by any means, electronic or mechanical, including photocopying and recording, or by an information retrieval system, must be obtained in writing from the publisher. Call or write Bard Press, an imprint of Longstreet Press, 2140 Newmarket Parkway, Suite 122, Marietta, GA 30067, phone 770-980-1488, fax 770-859-9894, or visit our website at www.bardpress.com.

ISBN: 1-885167-16-4 hardcover
ISBN: 1-885167-17-2 paperback

Library of Congress Cataloging-in-Publication Data

Farren, Caela.
     Who's running your career? : creating stable work in unstable
   times / Caela Farren.
          p.   cm.
     Includes bibliographical references and index.
      ISBN 1-885167-16-4 — ISBN 1-885167-17-2 (pbk.)
      1. Career development.   2. Job security.   3. Job satisfaction.
   I. Title.
   HF5381.F457   1997   97-23791
   650.1—dc21   CIP

To order additional copies of this title, contact your local bookstore or call (800) 229-5712.

The author may be contacted at the following address:
   MasteryWorks
   7353 McWhorter Place, Suite 200
   Annandale, Virginia 22003
   Phone (703) 256-5712, fax (703) 256-9564.

First Printing: August 1997
Second Printing: October 1999
Third Printing: December 2000

A BARD PRESS BOOK
Consulting Editor: Leslie Stephen
Developmental Editor: Jeff Morris
Word Processing Manager: Sherry Sprague
Copyeditor: Kathy Bork
Proofreaders: Deborah Costenbader, Doreen Piano
Cover Design: Hespenheide Design
Text Design/Production: Suzanne Pustejovsky Design
Text Composition: Round Rock Graphics
Index: Linda Webster

DEDICATION

For all working people—employed or in transition—

who know in their hearts

that there is a way to combine work and passion

and who are looking for guidance

in making that a reality in their lives.

For my mother and father,

who taught me the joy of work and contribution

at a very early age.

For Meaghan, my daughter, my friend,

who is my greatest supporter in work and in life.

For Marcia and Marilyn,

my friends and champions.

And for all young adults

who aspire to having stable work in these unstable times,

that they may choose and craft a mastery path.

Table of Contents

Acknowledgments

This book is the culmination of thousands of conversations with friends, family, clients, and colleagues about work and careers. I've watched great organizations collapse and new businesses succeed beyond their owners' wildest dreams. I've talked with hundreds of people about their sense of purpose, passion, fulfillment, joy, and confusion about work. I've counseled thousands of people who have been "downsized" and thousands more who are afraid it will happen to them. The system of work described in this book—the Web of Work—comes from all those sources. They are the inspiration for this book.

Peter Hartwick spent countless hours questioning, thinking, reading, and editing. Carol Willett was always there when I got writer's block or doubts about the importance of this work. Bev Kaye stimulated my interest in career development and collaborated with me in groundbreaking explorations. Fernando Flores helped me see the difference between jobs and professions and stimulated original thinking. Marc Young has been especially helpful in clarifying the dimensions of industries and jobs. Suzanne Eichhorn has given me unconditional support in writing this book.

I am grateful to the Sisters of Charity of the Blessed Virgin Mary, where I did my internship as an educator. Sister Mary Ellen Therese Barret showed me that passion for learning made learning possible. Birdie McElroy has been my staunch supporter, my greatest cheerleader, and my artistic adviser for thirty years. Jerry McElroy has been an avid reader and champion as well.

I am especially appreciative of colleagues who read and commented on the original draft of this book. Their insights, recommendations, support, and ideas have been incorporated throughout. Thank you, Susan Bassett, Rick Benner, Dede Bonner, Sharon Bray, Richard Dodson, Cindy Franklin, Heather Jacobs, Bonnie Maitlen, Cathy O'Neill, Anne Raftery, Wayne Reschke, Charlie Smith, Phil Smith, Deane Turner, and Jim Welch.

Recent work with the members of the Young Adults Mastery Club has given me a chance to test each of the concepts developed in this book. Thanks to all the young people in this club, who are committed to attaining mastery in their lives—Manuel Cruz, Zach Connelly, Cort Farrow, Bodhi Hagen, Dave and Adam Kreis, Gina Mendes, Nick Mertah, Meaghan Smith, and Sonia and Luis Vieira.

This book would not exist but for the powerful support of colleagues who have filled in for me, worked double time, and supported the importance of this work. They include Joyce Cohen, Cindy Gurne, Tom Karl, Janet Moynihan, Kathy Moynihan, and Jim Welch. Other associates have also contributed in a variety of ways. Thank you, Darlene Davis, Ted Fairchild, Jaye Smith, Penny Webb, and Mary Lou Zingale.

This book would also be nonexistent were it not for the expertise of the Bard Press team. Ray Bard believed in the book and taught me a lot about what makes for a great book. His entrepreneurial approach to publishing has been a fresh breeze. Leslie Stephen was masterful at telling me what I needed to hear in her first edit in ways that kept the wind in my sails and got the book more focused. Jeff Morris caught my passion and coupled it with his wealth of human experience; he brought breadth to these pages. Nancy Thomas has helped us all meet the day-to-day deadlines in bringing the book to fruition. Sara Schroeder tied all the loose ends together and made the final process easier with her uplifting confidence.

Last and by no means least, my gratitude goes to my daughter, Meaghan, who loves and admires the work I do and has stuck with me through all the late hours, early mornings, and millions of requests to "just listen to this" and "please read this just one more time." If this book helps Meaghan and her contemporaries craft professional niches for themselves, I will be a very happy woman.

Take Charge of Your Career

M AYBE YOU PICKED UP THIS BOOK because you feel out of control or unfulfilled. Or you are seeking "stability" in these seemingly chaotic and unstable times. Like millions of others, you'd like to have a sense of control and stability in your work life! You've chosen the right book! It will offer you the means to feel in charge and be in charge of "running your own career."

For the past twenty-five years I've been studying the question of career stability and work, and I assure you that once you begin to see the workplace patterns that I've discovered you *can* have a fulfilling and exciting work life! You will be able to see the stable underpinnings to the world of work and focus on those aspects of work that you *can* control. Contrary to the news reports we're bombarded with, not everything is changing. Twelve basic needs have given rise to nearly any work you can name. These needs have been around since the beginning of time, and will continue in some form for the foreseeable future.

My purpose in *Who's Running Your Career?* is to provide you a map—a system of work—so you can differentiate what *is* from what *is not* changing. You will learn to spot patterns in work and human life that are stable and enduring and which call for mastery-level skills. You will discover how to find more work than you could ever do in one lifetime, as long as you can deal competently with one or two basic needs—learning, family, leisure, economic security, or shelter—as the source of your work. Instead of worrying about work disappearing, you can focus your energy on building the kind of career that makes the world a better place for your having been here.

This book will give you confidence in exploiting opportunities as the world of work changes. You will be able to trace how change in one part of the picture impacts other areas and learn ways to detect those shifts before others. Change is accelerating—you can (and should) count on that! Let me be your guide and show you the places to look and the questions to ask that will give you confidence and competence to make the changes work *for* you rather than against you.

A World View

In the workshops I conduct as part of my consulting work, I ask people to cover their eyes and walk around the room. The results are as you might expect. People laugh nervously, breathe fast, take short, tentative steps and bump into things. When I ask them how they're feeling, they say, "Scared, tense, cautious, fearful, self-absorbed"—pretty much the same way they feel about the prospect of changing jobs, being downsized, and looking for work.

We depend on our view of the world around us—an almost unconscious awareness—to make our way confidently from place to place. Without that picture, we fear dangers both real and imagined. The more restricted our view the more we move hesitantly, clumsily, fearfully—or not at all. But with a clear view of our environs, we can navigate almost without thinking about it.

In some respects, the way most of us travel through our working lives—the learning, the jobs, the companies that hire us, the professions we pursue, the paths we choose—is like stumbling blindfolded through a strange room strewn with people, furniture, and other obstacles. We can sense the physical world around us, but our jobs, our careers, the ways we make our living are not real things in the physical sense—they are processes, actions, relationships, ideas. How can we find the clear pathways and navigate around obstacles that can't be seen, heard, or felt?

Wouldn't it be great if we could form a mental picture—a conceptual map—of the world of work? We would move more easily from one work situation to another, carrying our skills with us and applying them where they would do the most good for others and for ourselves.

The Web of Work

In my years of consulting experience in a wide variety of industries and companies, I have found that many, perhaps most, workers seem caught unaware when major changes—mergers, downsizing, outsourcing, acquisitions, layoffs—affect their organizations and their jobs. They react like the blindfolded walkers—tense, anxious, and uncertain of what to do next. Yet most of them are experienced workers with the skills and knowledge to weather the changes. With a clearer view of coming change, they could adapt with greater confidence rather than being forced into blind reactions. Yes, there are hazards in change, but also countless opportunities.

People in today's workforce are seeking an early warning to give them perspective on how to adapt—how to identify which industries are most in need of their skills and competencies, and which organizations are willing to pay well for their services. My quest for such a mental map and early warning system has resulted in the Web of Work.

The Web of Work

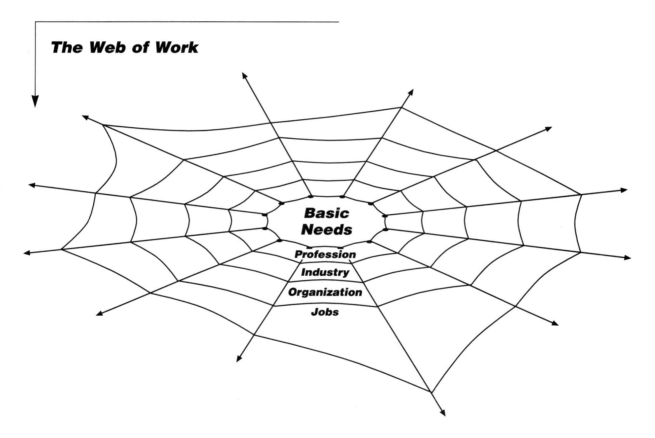

At the heart of this "map" are basic, unchanging human needs. This enclosed center is surrounded by successive rings that represent the ways in which human societies have learned to address those needs. These rings represent specialties or professions, groups of which combine to form industries. Those industries subdivide into organizations, which provide individual jobs. In subsequent chapters, you'll see how the Web of Work has been evolving since the beginning of civilization. The patterns through which work evolves are basically the same today as they were centuries ago.

The key to understanding the Web of Work is to trace how changes in any part of the Web cause vibrations elsewhere. The unchanging center is its most solid, stable part; the outer fringes—jobs—are the most fragile and unstable. This conceptual map mirrors the way the real world functions.

Stabilizing Your Career Path

While caution is wise, when an opportunity arises in our fast-changing, competitive world, you have to act quickly and surely. You have to take some risks, innovate, assert yourself confidently, even boldly. But it's hard to be bold when you can't see where you're going, where you've been, or what's around you. In such a situation, boldness is foolhardy. Unfortunately, this is the predicament in which most people who are "just doing their jobs" find themselves. How do you learn to navigate the shifting seas of career opportunity boldly and with assurance? Confidence comes from two sources: certainty and mastery.

Certainty comes from having the image of the Web in your mind, keeping it up to date, and staying alert to its fluctuations. The needs of industries and organizations change. Job requirements change. You have to watch all the connections, in all the rings of the Web, to see the changes coming. A small tremor in another ring on the far side can become a boom as it crosses the Web to where you are.

Mastery is a moving target; you have to keep updating your skills as technologies evolve. How does a new technology affect the way a profession addresses a basic human need? You may not only have to move to another position on the Web, but you may have to master new skills to stay there.

In the waning days of the twentieth century, these tremors are coming closer and closer together. New products, services, technologies, ideas, and behaviors are generating ever-larger shock waves that affect not just our own communities but the whole world. The outer, unstable parts of the Web—organizations and especially jobs—get the worst shaking. This book will help you connect with the inner, more stable parts of the Web, where your personal stability, professional mastery, confidence, and security lie. If you master professional skills and competencies that are valuable in many industries and organizations, you are attached securely to the Web in a way that you will not be shaken off, no matter how hard you are shaken.

My Plan to Increase Your Career Confidence

Each chapter gives you more details of the Web's structure. The further you read the more adept you will become at identifying both the various niches and the interconnections. You will be able to relate these to headlines about employment, television coverage of labor disputes, new product(s) on your supermarket shelf, and company downsizing with emerging demand, job offers, and career trends. You will see how the Web connects all these phenomena and which basics stay the same.

I have developed forty "Leading Career Indicators" (LCI), for exploring the factors that affect your career and identifying how they impact your career choices. Adapted from the federal government's Index of Leading Economic Indicators, the LCI helps you translate trends into choices. These indicators help you visualize the framework in which your career takes shape, just as Leading Economic Indicators help clarify the most significant factors that affect economic activity. Using the LCI, you will be able to recognize developing risks, assess potential opportunities, and weigh the critical factors that indicate whether your industry, organization, or profession is growing or shrinking. Mastering the factors that shape and influence your career, as well as our economic choices, is vital for two reasons. Having a context allows you to place yourself in the larger scheme of things and more importantly, allows you to exercise control in planning your life's work and charting your future.

Part I outlines how the Web of Work has evolved over the centuries and explains why it endures. It will introduce you to the forty Leading Career Indicators which you will use to assess the vitality of your profession, industry, organization, job, and measure your personal resilience.

Part II helps you explore the contribution you make to the world of work through your talents and gifts. You'll see the importance of knowing and appreciating your uniqueness and choosing a profession or trade that fulfills you. Eight indicators of personal mastery conclude part II.

Part III focuses on the enduring quality of professions and trades. You will assess your current stage of mastery and chart the steps for moving ahead. The eight indicators of professional vitality from part II will help you determine whether you are in the right industry, organization, and job to develop mastery in your profession or trade.

Part IV traces the evolution of industries and their importance as early warning signals of change. Compared with organizations and jobs, industries are stable and enduring. The question is, how well do you and your profession fit your industry?

Part V discusses organizations—where and how they fit in the Web of Work. Organizations change constantly in size and shape and many have short life spans. Choosing an organization that can be a partner in your professional development is more and more important. The indicators in this chapter illuminate what makes for a viable organization partner.

Part VI discusses the most fragile part of the Web of Work—the job. Because it is obviously associated with pay and employment, this is the ring of the Web that most people focus on. Choosing a job that supports ongoing mastery of your trade or profession is essential for your own employability. The indicators in this chapter will help you weigh both current and future job offers.

Part VII pulls the Web together and shows you how to create your own Capability Portfolio™. With a capable mindset, you'll see how to catch trends and anticipate niches for new work. You'll don entrepreneurial glasses to come up with ideas for new products or services you could offer—to your current organization, to competitors, or as the basis for your own business. You'll see how to generate products and services that meet the pressing needs of others.

Learning to orient yourself by using the Web of Work will enable you to analyze changes in your own work environment and separate the constant from the flux. As your confidence grows, you will no doubt see ways to create niches that are ideal showcases for what you do best. By basing your work on basic needs, you are assured of future demand for your contribution.

In short, you will be running your career.

Identify Your Stage in Work

Throughout the book, I've made special notes for three kinds of workers: new workers, people in transition from one job to another, and experienced workers. Each group faces different concerns, questions, assessments, and decisions. Read them all to fully benefit from this book, but pay special attention to the issues that concern you at your present career stage.

 ### New Worker
For the moment, consider yourself a new worker if you have recently graduated from high school or college, if you are now in your first job, or if you have worked less than five years. You may also find these notes useful if you are working part-time, holding a temporary job, or looking for work.

If you are a new worker, this book will help you

▶ see and traverse the entire Web of Work

▶ choose a profession or trade if you haven't already made that choice

▶ use the Leading Career Indicators™ to guide your choices of industries, organizations, and jobs

▶ assess yourself and find ways to express your unique talents

▶ see the value of choosing work environments where you can find mentors, learn powerful work habits and practices, and gain support in becoming a master in your profession

In Transition

You may be in transition if you are looking for work; considering another job, profession, or organization; bored or burned out, wondering if this is all there is to life; or thinking about following a dream you've avoided. Maybe you've been outplaced or downsized or right-sized or sense that you soon will be. Perhaps you just want to work for yourself, start your own business. Whatever the case, you're *in between* and wondering which way to jump.

If you are in transition, this book will help you

▶ see and understand what's stable and important in the Web of Work

▶ reevaluate your unique gifts and talents and see how you can serve others

▶ assess your past working situations against the Leading Career Indicators™ to gain insight on choices you've made

▶ determine what mastery level you've attained in your profession

▶ see ways to maximize your professional learning opportunities in a profession, industry, organization, or job

Experienced Worker

If you've been working for at least fifteen years and have mastered a profession or at least gained a reputation of competence or expertise, you're an experienced worker. You may well be someone others turn to for mentoring and career advice. Perhaps you feel that you could be contributing more or using your capabilities more fully. You might even be thinking of starting your own business, taking an idea that's been in the back of your mind for a long time and bringing it to fruition.

If you are an experienced worker, this book will help you

▶ assess and understand your own accomplishments and success in the Web of Work

▶ use the Leading Career Indicators™ to craft new and vital work opportunities for yourself

▶ coach and mentor younger colleagues who turn to you for advice and counsel

▶ decide whether you want to change the way you work to fit your other interests and hobbies better

▶ create a new business or new business opportunities

▶ spark ideas for new products and services

Whatever your career stage, there are many things you can do to maximize your benefit from this material. You'll learn more if you do the exercises, discuss your lessons and observations with friends and colleagues, and follow as many of the recommendations as time and inclination permit. You will also enhance your learning by reviewing the valuable books and articles listed in the bibliography.

I hope you derive as much benefit from this process as have many of my colleagues, clients, and acquaintances—and as I have in writing this book. I am sure you will gain some appreciation of the beauty of the Web of Work and the dignity and nobility of work itself in fulfilling our human needs. May this book help you feel more fully alive, proud of the contributions of your gifts and talents, and happy to be a cocreator of the Web of Work.

PART I

Needs Create Work,
Work Creates Opportunity

> **"Think not of yourself as the architect
> of your career but as the sculptor.
> Expect to have to do a lot of hard hammering
> and chiseling and scraping and polishing."**
> —*B.C. Forbes*

*I*f you're reading this book at a difficult time in your work life, you're not alone. More and more people are finding themselves in uncomfortable work situations, subject to the whims and wild weather of downsizing, outsourcing, merging, and other corporate storms. Perhaps you're wondering, How can I design my work life in a way to limit or foresee these stormy conditions?

In these two chapters you will learn about twelve basic human needs—among them leisure, shelter, health, family, work, economic security, and how these enduring needs generate work for humankind. You will discover how these needs are the origins of professions—how the need for efficiency and efficacy in taking care of necessi-

ties and desires led to specialization. You will see how groups of professions joined to become industries, how industries spawned organizations, and how organizations transformed the idea of work and created what we think of today as the job.

With these concepts in mind, you will learn that there are certain characteristics that indicate whether a job, an organization, an industry, or a profession has healthy prospects for survival and growth, and how those prospects affect your work life. Some indicators may apply to you personally and will indicate where your professional condition needs improvement.

Your introduction to the Leading Career Indicators™ will be tied to your career stage—whether you are a new *worker, in transition, or an experienced worker. This will show you how to apply the principles discussed in subsequent chapters.*

These first two chapters should be all the background you need to under-

stand personal values and vitality, professions, industries, organizations, and jobs. But if you wish to pursue these ideas further, remember to check the notes and reading list on pages 269–277.

Addressing Your Needs

2

Work and Life: What Counts for You?

The Evolving Web of Work

Tracking Changes in the Web of Work

*M*OST PEOPLE, WHEN CONSIDERING their work or career, look only at the narrow scope of their jobs. What most people fail to consider is that the centerpiece of our work system is service—service to our basic needs as people. In my consulting work over the past twenty-five years, I have identified twelve human needs that drive us as individuals and as a society. These needs haven't changed appreciably since the beginning of time. Professions, industries, organizations, and jobs continually evolve to satisfy one or more of these needs.

Here is the central premise of my Web of Work model:

There are twleve human needs that are timeless constants, that are at the center of our human experience. Professions, industries, organizations, and jobs exist and evolve to meet and satisfy one or more of these human needs.

But the needs themselves stay constant. The closer your work relates to providing food, shelter, leisure, entertainment, and so on, the more enduring and stable your work. The further removed your work is from addressing these basic needs (making T-shirts for people who already have everything, clerking three tiers removed from financial customers), the more unstable your work life is likely to be.

Twelve Human Needs

Home / Shelter

Family / Kinship

Work / Career

Social Relationships

Health—Physical and Mental

Financial Security

Learning

Transportation / Mobility

Environment / Safety

Community

Leisure

Spirituality

Advancements in society have improved our quality of life. However, they've also distanced us from the people and organizations that serve us and vice versa. Working people in large organizations sometimes forget *why* they're really working. They no longer see the real value they bring to the organization, or who benefits from their work. This is a warning sign. If you can't see, feel, and assess the results of your work, you are at risk.

Clarity about the needs that your job, organization, and profession serve contributes to both stability and security. The more directly you can deal with customers or clients, the better your sense of how important your skills are to others and what skills you need to develop to serve more powerfully. Without direct contact, work becomes a *job* rather than a *service*—and the motivation to improve erodes. Then, money rather than service of deep needs becomes the reward. When that happens, beware! You've lost the lifeline to continual learning.

None of us can satisfy all these needs ourselves. Others support us every day, both individually and collectively, in a variety of groups and settings. Our whole work system has developed to help us. Since the beginning of civilization, taking care of these needs has driven the formation of tribes, communities, cities, great inventions, and scientific breakthroughs.

Work and Life: What Counts for You?

As you review the list of twelve needs think about your career.[1] Which of the twelve has your work addressed? Are there certain needs that particularly interest you and move you to action? Any one of these can form the basis of a lifelong career, even in these days of change and uncertainty.

1. Home / Shelter.   To develop, maintain, and improve the structures and settings where we spend our lives—houses, apartments, offices, hotels, and the like—our civilization has developed a web of professions, trades, industries, organizations, and jobs focused on providing homes and shelter.

2. Family / Kinship.   Family concerns engage our creative energies daily. Some people are busy building families, taking care of parents or children, or repairing families after divorce, death, or marriage into extended families—and professions have sprung up to assist us with these tasks.

3. Work / Career.   Work is a form of expression through which we contribute to family and community. Our work may be paid or unpaid; we may train for a profession, trade, or craft and pursue it as our life's work, or we may work simply to earn a living. Succeeding in work gives one pride and a sense of contribution.

4. Social Relationships.   As social beings, we have to communicate and cooperate with other people to contribute to communities both local and global. In these times of high mobility and the alienation caused by living in large cities, we have developed elaborate outlets for social stimulation: restaurants, sports bars, athletic clubs, hobby groups, interest groups, church socials, community centers, and so forth.

5. *Health—Physical and Mental.* To be physically and mentally fit is the foundation for success in all other arenas. Personal health requires not only medical care but also proper diet, exercise, clothing, role models, and relationships. As people live longer, there is more and more emphasis on preventive rather than reactive health care and on caring for an aging population. Home health aides and retirement communities represent a sector of the Web of Work that is changing and growing rapidly.

6. *Financial Security.* The quest for financial security means managing resources to expand options and making decisions about income, budgeting, savings, investments, insurance, retirement, and other matters. The financial world continues to invent new ways to build, maintain, and manage financial security; meanwhile, many traditional financial service jobs are disappearing.

7. *Learning.* A uniquely human need is the quest to maintain and develop our intellectual capabilities by learning and applying new skills, knowledge, understanding, and wisdom. Hundreds of professions and thousands of organizations have evolved to help us learn.

8. *Transportation / Mobility.* We have learned the benefits of overcoming the restrictions of space, location, and time to pursue our interests and satisfy our needs. This desire has led from walking to horseback riding to automobiles to flight and, ultimately, to space travel. Phones, faxes, modems, the Internet, and teleconferencing have changed the conversation about mobility. It's now possible to "be" somewhere without actually going there. The nature of this human need is changing dramatically.

9. Environment / Safety.   A more recently recognized human need is to preserve, understand, and control the effects of the external physical world. Developed countries are concerned with controlling and repairing the damage that has resulted from many of our innovations in manufacturing, transportation, and other parts of the Web of Work. This is a class of work that will become more interwoven with other parts of the Web in the next two decades.

10. Community.   A central need of our civilization is helping others, volunteering, participating in politics, promoting justice, national and local security, and exercising social responsibility both locally and globally.

Our communities are the supportive cocoon in which we live and grow. Many agree that this part of the Web of Work has been badly neglected, the result being such things as drug abuse, the breakdown of the family, and underemployment.

11. Leisure.   A healthful lifestyle requires periodic regeneration of the mind and body. We renew our energy by diversifying our interests through sports, hobbies, vacations, and entertainment. This, too, is a thriving part of the work system, involving travel agencies, amateur baseball, cable TV, chat rooms on the Internet, virtual reality, craft stores, video productions, and many other opportunities.

12. Spirituality.   Humans have always explored the fundamental questions about the meaning of life through philosophy, humor, religion, the arts, and nature. This service sector helps us deal with the transcendent and holy in life. In this age of materialism, we are seeing a resurgence of interest in meditation, nature walks, outdoor challenge courses, and religion.

These twelve needs propel the evolution of our world and our own lives. Taking care of these needs is so habitual that we take our actions for granted. If you reflect for a minute on what you did yesterday, you will see that responding to these needs drove all of your actions.[2]

These needs not only drive much of our day-to-day existence, they also have caused the development of our professions, trades, crafts, organizations, support groups, jobs, and institutions. These needs are the core of human civilization.

The Evolving Web of Work

How does the Web of Work evolve to fulfill these basic human needs?

To test the proposition that these twelve needs motivate everything we do, let's examine one of them: *health.* As civilization has evolved from families to tribes to villages to cities to nations, taking care of our basic health needs has given rise to complex, multilayered, elaborate

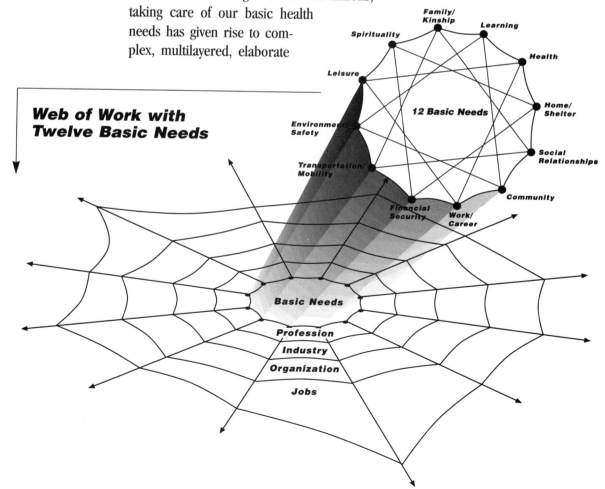

Web of Work with Twelve Basic Needs

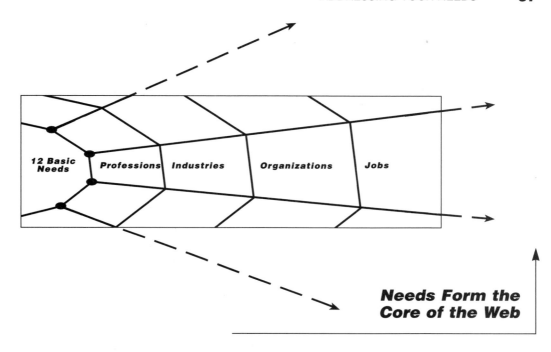

Needs Form the Core of the Web

systems. The more complex and specialized these systems have become, the further removed we have become from taking care of those needs personally.

Health Professions

In earliest times, shamans and designated tribespeople looked after the health needs of the tribe. Certain practices and rituals were passed down from generation to generation: dressing wounds, mending bones, gathering medicinal herbs, preparing for life changes. Tribal health specialists passed along their knowledge and rituals not to the tribe as a whole, but to members chosen by virtue of kinship, demonstrated talent, or supposed magical powers. This was the origin of medical practice.

As we've gained insight into our physical and mental health needs, more professions have emerged: surgeons, internists, dentists, chiropractors, geneticists, massage therapists, midwives, macrobiotic chefs, athletic coaches, ergonomic engineers, counselors, psychiatrists, and cosmeticians, to name only some. Specialties and individual jobs—phrenologist, alchemist, leech wrangler—appear and disappear over time, but the practice of health care, born in the dawn of humankind, grows stronger each year. Even some of the earliest medical specialties, such as midwifery and acupuncture, are still practiced today.

Professions in the Web

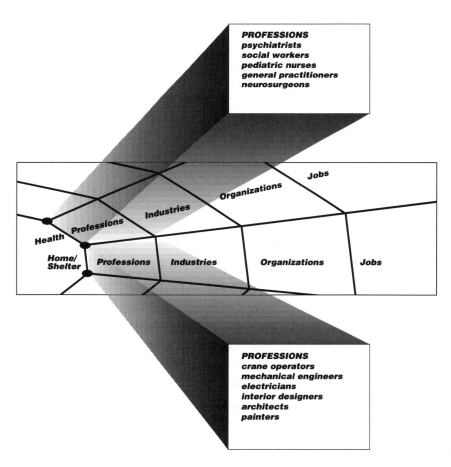

PROFESSIONS
psychiatrists
social workers
pediatric nurses
general practitioners
neurosurgeons

Jobs

Organizations

Industries

Professions

Health

Home/
Shelter

Professions   Industries   Organizations   Jobs

PROFESSIONS
crane operators
mechanical engineers
electricians
interior designers
architects
painters

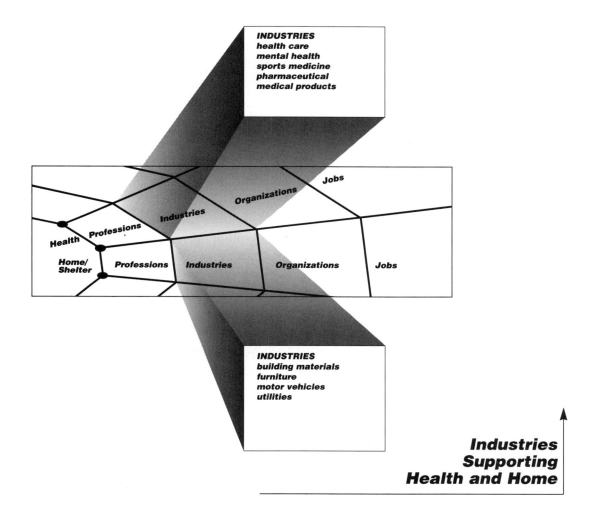

Health-Related Industries

To share experience, refine knowledge and technique, and advance technology, medical practitioners came together in organizations formed to promote their shared mission, taking care of their societies' physical and mental health needs. Guilds evolved into our present-day industry associations, such as the American Medical Association. These industry groups address a general human need, but are not necessarily exclusive; more than one industry group can be involved in any of the twelve basic needs. For example, transportation, education, and insurance are industry groups with an interest in physical and mental health, in addition to the other needs that they address. In terms of work, this makes professional opportunities available in more industries than you might otherwise expect.

The Web of Work shows industries emanating from professions. Professions are the most permanent, stable ring of the Web of Work, followed by industries. Industries do change, but they change more slowly than organizations and jobs, the two outer rings of the Web.

Health-Related Organizations

Organizations are formed when professionals come together to perform a specific function related to a human need. A health-related organization typically focuses on one or more specialties. Usually, the more specific the mission, the more successful the organization.

Today's health-care professionals can find work in thousands of organizations, from the National Institutes of Health to the American Red Cross, Mt. Sinai Hospital, McLean Health Club, Fairfax Rescue Squad, and Diets-to-Go.

Health-Related Jobs

Jobs—the outer circle of the Web of Work—are sets of related tasks or responsibilities within a profession, trade, or craft. As you'll see later in the book, jobs are the most fragile, transient part of the Web of Work. In fact, many jobs as we've known them are beginning to disappear. Project teams of multidisciplines are replacing many individual jobs.

Every human need is addressed by many people doing a variety of tasks. As a typical organization, such as a hospital, grows in size and complexity, it creates new jobs. Many of these jobs are directly related to the human needs being addressed (lab technicians, orderlies, nurses, nursing supervisors); others are support jobs, not specifically medical in nature

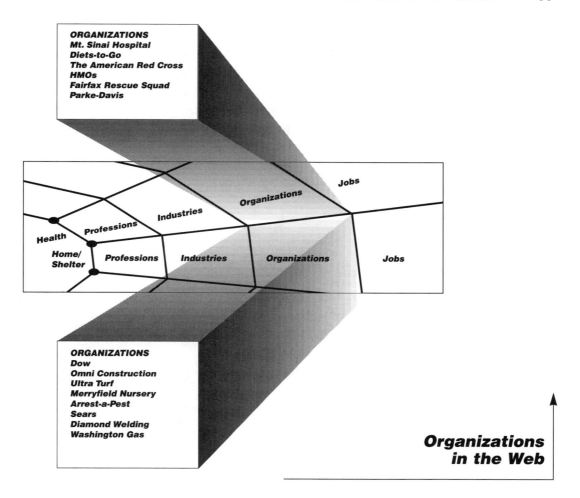

ORGANIZATIONS
Mt. Sinai Hospital
Diets-to-Go
The American Red Cross
HMOs
Fairfax Rescue Squad
Parke-Davis

Jobs

Organizations

Industries

Professions

Health

Home/Shelter

Professions

Industries

Organizations

Jobs

ORGANIZATIONS
Dow
Omni Construction
Ultra Turf
Merryfield Nursery
Arrest-a-Pest
Sears
Diamond Welding
Washington Gas

Organizations
in the Web

(administrators, laundry workers, schedulers, coffee shop managers). The industry itself may generate entire organizations that are not directly involved in the health of an individual, such as insurance companies and surgical supply distributors.

The explosive growth of health care as a competitive industry sometimes makes profits appear more important than patients. It is not unusual to deal with people who have very little knowledge or concern about the industry they serve, such as clerks, bookkeepers, customer service reps, and answering services. They're doing their jobs, but are often not even aware of the need they are helping to care for.[3]

In health care, as in other industries, revolutions in information and communication technologies are reducing the need for many support jobs. Organizations are downsizing and reengineering to reduce costs and stay competitive; most of the jobs that survive are those central to the mission of caring for the health of individuals.

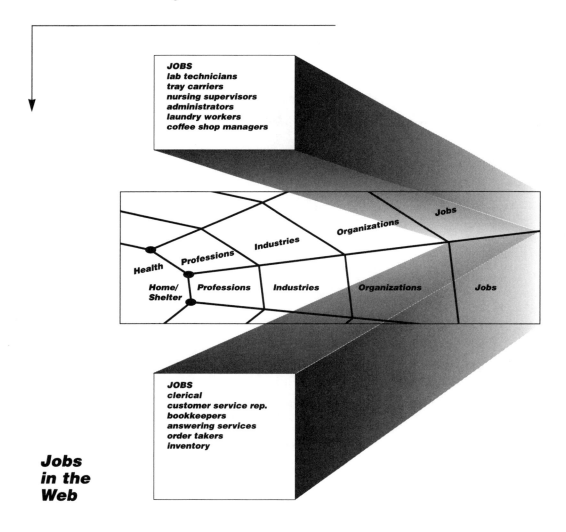

JOBS
lab technicians
tray carriers
nursing supervisors
administrators
laundry workers
coffee shop managers

Health
Home/Shelter
Professions
Industries
Organizations
Jobs

JOBS
clerical
customer service rep.
bookkeepers
answering services
order takers
inventory

Jobs in the Web

Tracking Changes in the Web of Work

The Web of Work is constantly changing, evolving, and reacting to outside factors. Like all complex systems, the entire Web reacts to changes to any of its parts. Technology breakthroughs in one profession or industry often affect how we take care of other human needs. The development of lasers for electronics, communications, and military purposes, for instance, has led to a revolution in some surgical procedures.

The Web of Work is a good metaphor for the system of work because it evokes the sense of intricacy, complexity, interconnectivity, and strength found in a spider web. As with a spider web, movement and activity in any part of the Web of Work will be felt throughout the rest of the Web. The spider is ever-vigilant to see that its web is strong, well-positioned in the environment, and capable of being quickly repaired or adapted if conditions change. So must we be.

In managing and designing our careers, it's essential that we develop a sensor network as sensitive and vigilant as the spider is for assessing all sectors of the Web of Work. When life was simpler, you could survive and thrive by simply paying attention to the job sector. Today you need to observe the entire Web of Work, the total system, if you want to be well positioned in your career.

The Forty "Leading Career Indicators"

OVER THE YEARS, I became more intuitive about what was happening in particular organizations, industries, and professions. Once I toured a medical supplies factory as part of my introduction to a new client who was looking for a systems approach to career development. In one large room I saw about fifty older women. All were doing the same thing, a task they had performed for twenty years or more: attaching suture threads to needles. I turned to my guide and asked, "Do those women know that in two or three years their jobs will be history?"

She gasped, "How do you know that?"

I was able to answer my host's question because, after this company invited me for a consultation, I began reading about problems and issues facing the health-care industry, the profession of surgery, and new medical procedures and technologies. I learned about endoscopic surgery, a less invasive way of removing or repairing internal organs with precision tools and miniature viewing devices. Endoscopic surgery not only helps patients recover faster but also slashes health-care costs by reducing surgical complications and shortening hospital stays. I realized that the new techniques would eclipse conventional surgery, and that trend would reduce, if not eliminate, demand for the suture needles the women made. I believed that these jobs would go the way of the buggy-whip craft—and they did, almost three years to the day after I toured the plant.

A Personal Map of the Web

In the twenty-five years I've been conducting career development conferences and workshops, I've been asked many questions by people concerned about their careers:

"Does my job have a future?"

"Will my kind of work be eliminated or outsourced?"

"Why won't my manager talk about the future of the company?"

"How can I know what I need to learn in order to stay competitive?"

Reflecting later on the experience at the medical supplies factory, I realized that my foresight came not only from my study of the company and its products but also from my unique perspective, a more general overview of industry trends and the interconnections among professions, industries, organizations, and jobs—the Web of Work. I had begun to construct my own mental map. The twelve basic needs and four sectors of work had become my investigative tools.

Then I began to wonder if I could identify indicators that could prove useful to people who wanted a more reliable career guidance system. I knew that people in the investment community used certain variables—their Leading Economic Indicators—to measure economic vitality, predict financial trends, and to guide their investment strategies. I wanted to see if we could employ the same type of precise indicators to build stable careers.

The Leading Career Indicators™

Countless business publications have formulated various indicators of health and risk in professions, industries, organizations, and jobs. Most, however, present a partial-systems view, focusing on only one or two aspects of work. Indeed, the people I've consulted usually focus only on their job, and rarely do they look as far as their organization. I wondered whether it was possible to develop a reliable way to assess the whole system.

I realized that you had to look at the entire Web of Work in order to speak with confidence about any one sector. Professions only have relevance within the context of the mission and strategies of a related organization. The health of an organization can be assessed only in terms of what else is going on in the industry. Job resilience can be assessed only by looking at the organization, changes in technology, and industry trends.

I wanted to design a tool that looked at the entire system of work. I wanted to be able to describe a reliable and systematic way to show people if and when their professions, industries, organizations, or jobs might be at risk in the next two to five years. My colleagues and I began looking for common themes, patterns of growth and decline, in each sector. Our research focused on the following questions:

► What did the best, most resilient industries have in common?

► How were the most-admired organizations described?

► Did the least-admired companies have anything in common?

► Which were the fastest-growing professions?

► Which were the fastest-growing or riskiest jobs?

► What were the characteristics of workers who seemed to rebound, no matter what happened to their job, organization, or industry?

The product of our three years of research is the Leading Career Indicators™ (LCI)—factors that anyone can use to assess the vitality of any sector of the Web of Work, including an individual job. For each of the five sectors of the Web, there are eight key indicators focusing on that sector. This interrelational aspect is important. People who use the LCI learn to view work as an interconnected system in which jolts to one part of the Web have implications on the others.

Our research also showed us that some sectors of the Web of Work are more fundamental, more enduring, than others—especially professions. Choosing a profession, trade, or craft is the most important work decision you will make. Industries, organizations, and jobs have evolved over time to house the life work of the professions, trades, and crafts that have evolved from our twelve basic human needs. Once you've settled on a profession, your choices of industry, organization, and job type become clearer.

Exploring the Leading Career Indicators™

Where do you start a career inquiry? Where do you concentrate your efforts? You can briefly survey the indicators in this chapter to get a good idea of where you need to concentrate your energy at work or in your career search inquiry. Quickly scan each of the indicators and give a preliminary "yes" or "no" to each one. The indicators will give you different guidance, depending on whether you are just starting a career, looking or being compelled to change jobs or careers, or experienced and successful but looking for new challenges. But first, identify yourself as a New Worker, In Transition, or Experienced Worker using the descriptions that follow.

New Worker

Use these indicators to help you select the professions, industries, organizations, and jobs where you're most likely to succeed. If you haven't chosen a profession, select one that you are considering and use it as the reference point for answering the questions. If you haven't selected a specific industry or organization, review the questions for the ones you are contemplating. If you're researching a specific job, use the job indicators to guide your queries. If you don't have the experience you need to answer some of the questions, ask them when you interview. At this stage, you should look for strong yeses to the indicators for industry and profession. Concentrating on these will help you choose wisely.

In Transition

If you've been outplaced recently or had your job "reengineered" out of existence, answer the LCI by using your latest organization and industry as the reference point. This may give you some ideas about why you were let go, and insights that will make it easier to avoid repeating patterns. If you've got a job but are having doubts about it or thinking of changing jobs, you can use the questions as indicators of your potential in new parts of the Web of Work. In this quick review, you'll learn where you were most at risk with your last employer— at the profession, industry, organization, or job level. Some of the indicators can serve as questions you can ask about prospective work situations.

Experienced Worker

In scanning the indicators, you will probably see why you've been successful in your career. If you've worked in more than one profession, industry, or organization, reflect on each and answer accordingly. As you think about new work opportunities, use the questions in each sector to guide your research and inquiries.

If your response is "yes" for six of the eight indicators in each sector, you're on the right track; four or fewer should serve as an early warning—a call for immediate, effective career action. Viewing your career in the context of the larger Web of Work will give you more control, perspective, leverage, and flexibility for running your career intelligently.

EIGHT INDICATORS OF PERSONAL VITALITY

1. **Chosen a profession**

2. **Exceed your work expectations**

3. **Continue to learn your entire life**

4. **Appreciate differences in culture, style, and so on**

5. **Use computers and technology**

6. **Demonstrate mastery in one or more areas**

7. **Initiate work projects**

8. **Work closely with customers**

Individual Indicators

Regardless of where you are working, there are several indicators that reliably predict your future employability. If you are not working full time, these indicators will quickly demonstrate your readiness to make major contributions in work. You can also use your prior part-time work, school, and extracurricular activities to bolster your employability as a future worker. We will discuss a variety of ways to assess your passion, personality, and profession in part II.

Profession Indicators

Professions change constantly—but they endure. Engineers have been around since tribal times. Mechanical engineers made the first tools; construction or civil engineers made the first lodges and bridges. Health-care specialists evolved from the early shamans, herb collectors, and midwives. Professions come from our basic needs. Think about your own profession, or one you are considering, and mentally tick off "yes" or "no" for each indicator.

Some questions for reflection:

► Have I chosen a profession, trade, or craft? Which one?

► Which of the twelve human needs does my profession address?

► How does this profession relate to my personal passion and interests?

► What professional associations are available for networking and support?

► With whom could I discuss my answers to the above questions?

Part III will show you the importance of choosing and mastering a profession.

Industry Indicators

Industries are informal groups of professionals working together to take care of one or more human needs. As the world economic system evolved, professionals (hunters, artisans, builders, cooks, and so on) came together in groups and guilds to learn from each other and pass accumulated knowledge to succeeding generations. These groups and guilds formed the basis

EIGHT INDICATORS OF PROFESSION VITALITY

1. **Essential to the purpose of the organization**

2. **Transfers to other industries and organizations**

3. **Competencies apply to other professions**

4. **Provides financial and personal compensation**

5. **Professional associations exist**

6. **Obvious path to mastery**

7. **Age-independent**

8. **Requires communication outside the organization**

of our modern industry and trade associations, which help us develop professionally and assess our competitors.

Questions for reflection:

▶ In which industry do I now work? In which others have I worked?

▶ What human need(s) does it address?

▶ What social, political, technical, or economic trends will affect the industry?

▶ Is my profession or job required for the industry to achieve its mission?

Joining industry associations or reading industry journals will help you see the big picture and patterns in your industry. The trends that are already affecting your profession, organization, and job will make more sense in the context of your industry. Part IV will give you a better understanding of how to assess an industry and actions you can take to stabilize your work.

EIGHT INDICATORS OF INDUSTRY VITALITY

1. **Serves an important need**

2. **Keeps up with changing technologies**

3. **Demonstrates high-growth potential**

4. **A variety of professional niches**

5. **Globally competitive**

6. **Locally competitive**

7. **Minimal regulations**

8. **Continues to expand products and services**

Organization Indicators

Organizations are temporary systems; they are the second most fragile part of the Web of Work. Organizations come into being when someone states a specific goal or mission and invites others to work together to achieve those results. Examples might be the following:

"Let's start a car pool."

"Would you work with me to raise money for cancer research?"

"Let's have a computer in every home."

These needs were either so urgent or so intriguing that people banded together to fulfill them. Thus were born the St. Thomas Aquinas High School car pool, the American Cancer Society, and Apple Computer. Thousands of organizations are born and die every day.

Questions for reflection:

▶ What is the mission and strategic direction of my organization? What is the mission of my contemplated organization?

▶ Who are my organization's major competitors?

▶ What trends and problems currently affect my organization?

▶ How is my organization preparing for the future?

Part V will develop these themes more fully. You will see much more clearly whether your organization has a strong future, or how organizations you are thinking of joining stack up.

EIGHT INDICATORS OF ORGANIZATION VITALITY

1. **Sense of purpose**

2. **Leaders come from core professions**

3. **Conducts research and development**

4. **Demonstrates growth potential**

5. **Learning culture**

6. **Wealth sharing**

7. **Information sharing**

8. **Power sharing**

Job Indicators

A job is a temporary way to package a task that needs to be done for an organization to achieve its mission. During the Industrial Revolution, we took professions and broke them into bite-sized pieces of work—jobs—that "unskilled" laborers could do. As industries evolve or organization missions change, jobs are the first part of the work system to be reorganized, outsourced, or eliminated. Although professions might be outsourced to another company specializing in a service, they are not eliminated. Jobs, on the other hand, are the least stable element in the Web of Work. This sector requires continuous vigilance.

EIGHT INDICATORS OF JOB VITALITY

1. **Crucial to organization mission**

2. **Enhances and requires mastery**

3. **Works closely with the customer**

4. **Creates visibility in the profession**

5. **Growth options in industry**

6. **Longevity**

7. **Fits values and interests**

8. **Provides a service to others**

Questions for reflection:

► What professional development opportunities are available in my current job?

► How will industry trends change my job?

► How will organizational change affect my job?

► Will my job be needed in the next two to five years?

The more your job contributes directly to the mission of the organization or to customer satisfaction, the longer it will probably last. It's only a matter of time, however, before most jobs disappear or are reorganized as different competencies and skills are required. Successful careerists see their jobs in the context of the larger organization, industry, and profession. Part VI will give you many ways to view this facet of the Web of Work.

Part II highlights the importance of knowing yourself and appreciating your unique talents. Certain personal attributes, if developed, will increase your confidence and competence in life and work.

Mastering the Web of Work

The more "yes" answers you've made to the LCI, the more likely you are to have stable and fulfilling work in your future. The possibilities are without limit—restricted only by your imagination. It's up to you to take charge of your own learning and level of professional mastery.

Part VII will help you pull all your learning together and find all the niches where you can make your best contributions. We'll give you plenty of tips on how to maximize your talents and become marketable now and for the future.

In the rest of the book, we will bring each of these indicators to life. You will receive guidance and tips on steps you can take to develop a stable and resilient work life. We'll start by focusing on you—your passion, purpose, and unique talents.

PART II

Passion, Purpose, and Career

"People cannot find their missions
until they know themselves."

—Laurie Beth Jones

Not so long ago, work was intimately associated with what kind of person you were and what your natural inclinations and talents led you to do for the community—blacksmith, midwife, seamstress, farmer, doctor, and so on. Work and service were more closely linked. Natural talents were the links.

The Industrial Revolution and mass production spoiled that convenient arrangement. Factories employed thousands of workers. People left behind the hard and uncertain life of making a living in a small community to take dull but reliable factory jobs in cities. One job was much like thousands of others; employees were considered interchangeable parts—movable, but more or less permanent. Unique talents and personal aspirations were lost by many.

Workers came to believe that they must join some organization in order to survive, succeed, and provide for their families. People lost their sense of self-sufficiency and confidence that they had the resources within to provide value to their community and earn a living by doing so. Lost also was the day-to-day routine of caring for and supporting neighbors and being supported by them in turn. Work revolved more around money and status than service or community.

Having to leave home to find work makes people lose touch not only with their families and communities but also with their natural strengths, inclinations, and desires. The few who manage *to keep this insight often come to believe they don't have what it takes to follow their bliss. Instead, many follow someone else's and slowly lose their spirit, their connection with their true values and unique gifts. Today, people's spirits are being snuffed out because they have lost sight of their inner purpose and drive. Employees who are offered only a part of a job to do are never given the opportunity to develop mastery. People don't feel comfortable or confident in the workforce if they haven't mastered something.*

In recent years, however, economic and technological changes are leading a return to more positive ways of working. New work structures are

New Worker

▶ *Part II is a must-read section for you! Appreciating, honoring, and fulfilling your true self is the foundation from which you can make sound career decisions. On this knowledge you will be able to build a successful and personally meaningful career based on your inner talents.*

In Transition

▶ *Ask yourself, "Why am I in transition?" Are you facing external changes at work or are you responding to a festering dissatisfaction with the work you've been doing? In either instance, you can seize this opportunity to gain clarity about your talents and where you would like to apply them.*

Experienced Worker

▶ *The more masterful you've become, the truer you are already to yourself and others—but perhaps you haven't yet fulfilled your dreams. This section will provide you new insight that will help you live even more fully, to create or find work that better fulfills your inner calling.*

beginning to restore a sense of our unique abilities and natural inclinations. These new work structures point the way to successful, satisfying work lives that let our entrepreneurial spirit thrive once more. Motivating us to take advantage of these alternatives is the ever-growing wave of corporate restructuring. Our initial reactions to having our job disrupted are to be angry and to panic about our future. But to move forward, we must look beyond our pain and assess our position in the workplace. Helping others make this assessment in a systematic manner is my mission in teaching seminars and writing this book.

Being "downsized" out of a job has a way of focusing your mind— once you've gotten past the anger and panic—on what you want to do. You can contract your services, work experience, and skills to other buyers, sometimes even your former employer. You can cultivate the talents you've heretofore neglected and sell those to the highest bidders. You can fulfill your dream of parking your car semipermanently and working at home in T-shirt and shorts. The fact that over 45 million Americans now work from home suggests that people can once again focus on their natural talents, affinities, and goals.

4

Learn to Live Your Passion

I HAVE BEEN ENCOURAGING YOU to examine your work and career from a new perspective. My hope for all my clients and readers is that they find their inner calling, or what "makes their heart sing." But if this is all new to you, how do you go about identifying and discovering the power of your personal attributes—that combination of *your* innate strengths, talents, and inclinations that will result in a passion in you for a particular type of work?

In Hinduism and Buddhism, *dharma* is the ultimate law of things—their essential nature. The dharma of a fire is to burn; of the wind, to blow. To answer the question "Who are you?" you must discover your dharma. What is your essential nature? When you are respecting your dharma, you are pursuing your "right livelihood." Keep in mind that there is at least one thing you can do better than anyone else in the universe. Find it!

I was recently asked to coach a successful entrepreneur who was in some emotional turmoil about whether to keep or sell her business. I asked her to describe for me the times when she was happiest in life. She answered readily: when she was having fun, being intellectually challenged, mentoring, moving around, enjoying a great deal of variety, and contributing to a team. In her current business, which she and a friend had started, she felt most of these joys were missing. She was feeling depressed, burned out, lifeless. In the truest sense, she was no longer able to be herself, and she didn't like the person she was becoming. Upon reflection, she saw that the only reason she was holding on was for financial security, and that the price was her sense of peace and contentment. She decided to sell the business and find or create a new setting where she could be herself.

Accentuating the Affirmative

Discovering your dharma—emphasizing your innate talents and inner calling—is contrary to much of today's conventional wisdom. Current popular theorists promote "personal development" that focuses on correcting weaknesses to complement strengths. Notable exceptions are Donald Clifton and Paula Nelson, who, in their book *Soar with Your Strengths,* argue for focusing on strengths and developing mastery and excellence around them instead of becoming preoccupied with weaknesses.

John came to our WorkPower™ workshop four years ago. I noticed him immediately. He looked like he had been badly traumatized—pale, no light in his eyes, disinterested. We did an exercise where people examined where they had been and where they wanted to be. As John spoke, his body began to change. He sat up. Color came back to his skin. His eyes came alive. I asked him what had happened and he told me that eight years before he had taken a management position, much against his own better judgment. But his family, friends, and boss had all pressured him to accept the promotion. He had been a technical leader in the computer company, but had always felt like a failure as a manager. His mental shift came when he realized that his passion was in his technical prowess. After the workshop, he went back to his boss, took a demotion to his original position, and now is much happier. John realized that emphasizing his strengths—technical mastery—was more important than money or prestige. By making the shift, he was running his career.

Who *Are* You?

It's never too late to start developing your talents. The more you can weave your work web around your strengths, the more productive and happy you will be.

To begin, take a few minutes and try the following exercises:

▶ Ask three or four friends or family members what they most value about you.

▶ Ask yourself what you cherish most about yourself. What is your core? What are your unique gifts?

▶ Find a picture that represents you or a metaphor that best expresses you.

You may be surprised at how similar your loved ones' responses are—and how satisfying it can be to discover that your dharma is understood and appreciated.

Stop for a few minutes and list the traits that you and others would use to describe you. Scan the list of personality traits for ideas; write down those that best describe you.

Next, call or fax a request to five or six people who know you well. Ask them the following:

▶ What five or six words would you use to describe me?

▶ If your best friend asked you to tell her more about me, what would you say?

▶ What do you see as my driving force? What makes me tick?

Personality Traits

Analytical	Hands-on	Quick
Artistic	Inquiring	Quiet
Candid	Low-key	Rational
Caretaking	Loving	Relaxed
Creative	Open	Serious
Diplomatic	Outgoing	Slow
Emotional	Persevering	Thoughtful
Firm	Pessimistic	Upbeat
Funny	Physical	Uptight
Guarded	Proud	Warm

Your friends and family can give you other words that will probably validate many of the words you've already written to describe your style or personality.

A key factor in finding your best career niche and mastering a profession is to choose work that fits your personality. If you are talkative, charismatic, and optimistic, you might be great in sales, education, or customer service. If you are good with your hands, creative, sociable, and color savvy, your career niche might be interior design, art instruction, or fashion. The more you can match your own inclinations to the characteristics of the industry and profession you join, the more energy you will have to put into the work itself.

What Interests You?

Part of your dharma has to do with the things you like to do. Pay attention to what turns you on. What activities interest you? How do you like to spend your time? If your work life involves the things you really like to do, you'll probably derive great satisfaction from doing your work well—like the painter who captures her feelings on canvas, the child whose Lego building looks like the one in his mind, and the teacher who sees her student suddenly grasp a new idea.

People's intrinsic interests seem to lie in one or more of these four basic areas:

- ▶ People
- ▶ Ideas
- ▶ Data
- ▶ Things

I've found these categories helpful in guiding people who are not exactly sure what they want to do.

Recently I was talking with my daughter's eighteen-year-old friend Luis about his goals and whether being an auto mechanic would really suit him. My daughter Meaghan got out our Deal Me In deck,[1] each card of which describes an activity such as selling, repairing, building, inventing, or analyzing. She asked Luis to shuffle it and pull out the ten cards of things he most enjoyed doing. Luis did so without hesitation. Eight of his ten involved working with things; the other two, people. When he read the card listing occupations that would suit him, auto mechanic was one of the first on the list. Luis beamed and said, "Someday I'm going to own my own shop." And I'm sure he will.

For any industry, you can brainstorm a list of jobs and professions for those who love to work with people, with ideas, with information, or with physical objects. You can also survey your current organization for other jobs in your interest category, or for ones that mix two interest categories. Don't confuse your natural interests with your acquired skills. It's possible to be good at something but not love it. Satisfaction always includes feelings of pride, joy, excitement, and gratitude. If you don't feel satisfied, you're probably not building on a strength.

What Do You Care About?

Values are those things we cherish or aspire to in our lives. They give us a sense of meaning and fulfillment. Recognizing these values is an important part of becoming your own person. As children, we are surrounded and influenced by outside values—those of our family, friends, community, religion, and culture. As mature adults, we review and confirm our own values as distinct from those of our formative influences. Some values are more important to us than others; we need to recognize this fact and keep our values in mind when choosing partners, teammates, workplaces, and professions. Being in harmony with our values is important for both our physical and our spiritual health.

Examine the following list of values. Choose the ten that are most important to you—both at work and at home. If other values are important to you, add them to the list.

What Is Your Mission in Life?

The people who derive the most joy and satisfaction from their careers can usually describe their work in terms of a personal mission. To know your mission, you must first know yourself. As your unique talents and strengths become apparent to you, you can seek a way to meet the needs of the community by performing work that is a natural expression of your mission.

For years I have said that my mission is to "create environments where people can be more than they ever dreamed." This has also been the mission of my company. More and more, however, I see this mission transcending all the boundaries in my life. My main concern, whether I'm looking at my daughter and her friends, my home, my company, my teaching, or any relationship, has become centered on one question: "Is my environment opening people to new possibilities?"

Stating your mission is a challenge. Writing it down and sharing it with others makes it real and commits you to doing what you say. Whenever my mission or purpose has been blurred or in transition, I have felt depressed, unfocused, tired, unskilled, and afraid. Having a sense of purpose makes me eager to get up in the morning and gives me a way to assess my contribution at day's end.

Laurie Beth Jones, in her book *The Path,* has developed an amazing exercise for helping people explore and express their sense of purpose. She asks you to decide which of the elements

*P*ersonal Values

Accomplishment	Humor
Acknowledgment	Independence
Adventure	Initiative
Artistic expression	Integrity
Athletic	Intelligence
Autonomy	Leading
Balance	Learning
Beauty	Money
Being the best	Nature
Challenge	Power
Collaboration	Resourcefulness
Competence	Respect
Emotion	Security
Excitement	Self-expression
Family	Service
Freedom	Social relationships
Friends	Solitude
Fun	Teamwork
Giving	Variety
Honesty	Warmth / love

of classical Greek natural science you are most like—earth, air, fire, or water—and to write twelve characteristics describing that element. I chose water, which I see as cleansing, refreshing, life-giving, moving, changing, relentless, powerful, transparent, multifaceted, and so on. The other elements might bear the following descriptions: Fire is hot, sporadic, warming, fueling, intense, and ever-changing. Earth is stable, grounding, steady, yielding, and strong. Air is invisible, life-giving, and responsive. I was amazed at how these descriptors helped me view my own talents and uniqueness. I was excited by the beauty and power of the exercise. When I asked others who know me well what element they would have chosen to describe me, all said water, for many of the same reasons. This exploration opened a powerful dialogue in me and showed me the kinds of work I needed to be doing more of and less of.

Jones has a series of steps, based on three factors, that help you develop a mission:

▶ What you do

▶ Why you do it

▶ Where you do it

The exercise helped me pull together the concepts of dharma (being) and vocation (calling to service), to focus on what I felt was a crying need in contemporary America: to inspire, advance, and support mastery in young adults. It restored my sense of direction, passion, and confidence and gave me a vision for my work for the next decade. Out of this was born not only my mission but my new company name: MasteryWorks™.

Take a few minutes to reflect on what you stand for:

▶ What do you want to achieve in your life?

▶ What values or issues do you care deeply about?

▶ What people or situations do you wish to affect?

Write down a synopsis of your mission. Make it clear enough to serve as a compass for your day-to-day life. Examples:

"Encourage creativity in children."

"Assure quality of life for older people."

"Mentor start-up businesses for female entrepreneurs."

"Encourage self-sufficiency in school dropouts."

"Bring pride to new immigrants."

"Foster beauty and relaxation in my home."

What Are You Passionate About?

Joseph Campbell extolled the importance of "following your bliss," your dreams, the inner voice that urges you to do what is uniquely yours to do. Another word for bliss is *passion,* the life force that compels you, regardless of obstacles, to use your heart, mind, hands, and will to make something happen or to bring something into being—to excel on the parallel bars, design the perfect kitchen, write the Great American Novel, operate the best foreign car repair shop in town, or find the magic bullet against cancer.

Following your passion can be simultaneously selfish—the bliss of total absorption, the emphasis on personal fulfillment—and selfless—the joy of sharing a purpose with others, providing vast benefits to your community and the world. Passion and purpose go hand in hand. Passion is the emotional energy, the fire in the belly, the willpower, the courage you harness to achieve your mission despite all obstacles and reversals.

You can see both purpose and passion in

▶ teachers who inspire students to create award-winning science projects, perform in plays, and master foreign languages

▶ customer service people who won't stop until they meet your needs and assure your satisfaction

▶ athletes who gain confidence through their relentless pursuit of excellence

▶ engineers who worked twelve years to get Project Galileo to Jupiter

▶ advocates for the homeless who volunteer to create shelters, lobby politicians, and teach less-fortunate people to take care of themselves again

▶ artists like Georgia O'Keeffe, who was still painting in her eighties and helping shape the world of art, or Miró, who created some of his best-known works while bedridden

▶ people you have known in your life or career (How many can you name? What are their passions? What were their contributions? Which of the twelve basic needs are they serving? What is it like to be around them?)

Passionate people don't spend much time talking about how awful the world is, how unfortunate they are, or how difficult it is to keep learning and improving. They are much more intent on achieving their dreams and goals than on feeling bad about the effort it takes to achieve them.

Here's a revealing exercise. On a sheet of paper, write down times in your life when you felt passionate, had a clear sense of purpose, were moved to accomplishment, and were happy and proud as a result. Notice what you feel when you start plugging into your accomplishments: probably joy, a surge of energy, a release, a sense of hope and courage. Go back to your list and add other examples; put in a few more details:

▶ What were you doing?

▶ Whom were you with?

▶ What strengths were you using?

Close your eyes and see if you can picture any other achievements. Don't rush; relax and let your emotions lead you in painting a clear picture of your strengths. Note the images, feelings, and insights that emerge from this exercise. Circle the accomplishments that seemed to become clearer and more focused.

Seeking to understand your unique talents leads you to your passion. Passionate moments are those when you and the world are in harmony, when there's little or no conflict between your inner strength and goals and the outer world. This harmony often leads to satisfaction and mastery.

According to Tod Barnhart, a successful broker and now a personal wealth guru, "seeking our dreams is discovering what you love so much that you'd do it for free. When you identify whatever that is, and do it well and with passion and commitment, the world responds like you've never imagined."[2]

Mastery of any profession or craft requires ongoing learning. What do you learn quickly and most easily? If you can catch on fast, jump in, practice, and succeed, chances are you're learning in one of your strengths. A strength is always characterized by initial rapid learning as well as continual learning throughout one's lifetime. If this isn't true for you in your daily work, self-examination may be in order.

A coach or mentor can speed up our learning by helping us design a learning path that includes

- ▶ basic practices and tools to master

- ▶ competencies and skills to acquire

- ▶ measures of effectiveness

- ▶ must-read books, articles, or journals

- ▶ problems to solve that help you grasp the basic principles and practices

- ▶ other people to know and to whom your work must be known

Coaches help us progress along the learning curve by showing us what's important and what's not. We can then concentrate on developing knowledge and skills rather than wasting our time on learning and practicing the wrong things.

I learned the value of an expert coach in 1986. On New Year's Eve, I was forty-five years old. As I thought about my resolutions, I knew I had to get in better shape. Though I had never run a race in my life, I declared to a couple of runner friends that I would run the 10K Bonne Belle race that May. My friend Kathy had run many 10Ks; she said she would train with me. Her friend and fellow runner, Bill, said he'd be my coach. Bill told us how far and how long to train each week. I followed his instructions faithfully (even though I often disagreed with them; left to my own counsel, I would have run faster, longer, harder, earlier—and probably would have quit). With my friends and family cheering me on, I ran my first 10K and achieved my goals: to finish the race and to come in far from last. I knew that the only reasons I had done so well in my first race were Bill's coaching and Kathy's support. That was the end of my "Lone Ranger" approach to learning.

Mastery in any job, profession, or activity shows up in action and accomplishment, not merely in knowledge. Coaches help us practice the skills required for mastery. Finding a great coach or mentor is a gift to be sought out. These are the musts for rapid learning in the new millennium: a specific mission that arouses your passion and a talented mentor who can guide your learning.

Individual Resilience Indicators

5

*H*OW RESILIENT ARE YOU? No matter where you work, what you do, or where you are in your professional development, there is a way of measuring how well you can withstand, adapt to, and profit from changes in the workplace. I have selected eight characteristics that I believe most strongly predict how flexible and adaptable you are in the work world. I call these "individual indicators" (see box on page 75). Each of these characteristics contribute to personal resilience in your career and help make you highly valued in any industry or organization.

Choose a Profession

The Industrial Revolution created an enormous, continuing demand for semiskilled workers. It also created the illusion that workers need not be concerned about professional considerations. Excellence—the mastery of a craft or trade—has faded from the general scene, however, and is now found mainly in specialties and custom work.

Becoming excellent, a master craftsperson or professional, is one of the highest forms of human achievement. Others in your profession come to you for help, learning, leadership, and coaching. You are respected by your peers and colleagues within your current work setting and, usually, beyond.

Here are some questions to think about:

► Have you chosen a profession in which to excel?

► Who are the best in your profession?

► What would it take to work with them, study them, learn from them?

► If you've not yet chosen a profession, which ones interest you?

Part III will show you how and why to excel in a profession.

Exceed Work Expectations

Gil Hammond is one of the best managers I've ever known. Gil builds factories. He builds them ahead of schedule, under budget, anywhere in the world, with people who would give almost anything to work with him again. How does he do it? He finds out what everyone involved in a project expects—employees, construction companies, managers, vendors—and he lets them know what he expects. He asks them the following questions:

▶ What do I need to do more of for success?

▶ What do I need to do less of for success?

▶ What do I need to continue doing?

▶ What do I need to prepare for?

Your career is fortified when people know what to expect of you—and you make it a practice to exceed those expectations. First, communicate regularly with customers, team members, and supervisors. Learn what others expect of you and let them know what you want of them. Don't take anything for granted; work changes fast, and so do priorities. Clarify your priorities and expectations regularly.

Once you're clear on what's expected of *you,* exceed those expectations. You are most likely to exceed expections if you are a professional, dedicated to excellence, driven by passion, purpose, and your own high standards. Not exceeding expectations should be a red flag to you; perhaps you are in the wrong job or line of work.

Ask yourself the following:

> **EIGHT INDICATORS OF PERSONAL VITALITY**
>
> 1. **Choose a profession**
> 2. **Exceed work expectations**
> 3. **Continue to learn**
> 4. **Appreciate differences**
> 5. **Use information technology**
> 6. **Demonstrate mastery of a chosen profession**
> 7. **Initiate work projects**
> 8. **Work closely with customers**

▶ What do I expect of myself?

▶ What do others expect of my day-to-day performance?

▶ When do I exceed my own and others' expectations?

▶ When do I fall short? Why?

> ▶ What else could I contribute that would add value for my customers?

Current performance is the doorway to future options. Even if you're in a temporary job or haven't yet found your profession of choice, work done well is a source of pride, confidence, and respect. Don't let your job description limit your commitment. "That's not my job" should never pass your lips.

Keep Learning

Being prepared for the new millennium requires both the confidence of an accomplished professional and the curiosity of a child. You can't rely on what you know; to stay ahead in your career, you must always be learning. Take nothing for granted. Cultivate the art of questioning. Questions uncover old patterns, bad habits, and mistakes. They generate new connections, new concepts, new paradigms—and new ways to anticipate change and adapt our work.

Regularly ask such questions as:

> ▶ When did people start asking for this product or that service?

> ▶ Who are the best in this profession, task, project, service?

> ▶ What does it take to be the best?

> ▶ What new competencies or skills will be needed?

> ▶ What new learning will be required on my part?

Today we have access to a wide variety of learning technologies: audiotapes, videotapes, online learning, CD-ROMs, chat rooms, books, magazines, journals, and long-distance learning. If you know what you want to learn, you'll find few obstacles to learning it.

Appreciate Differences

In these days of rapid worldwide transportation, immigration, communication, and commerce, we live in an unavoidably multicultural, multilingual world. Our customers, colleagues, and competitors grow more diverse every day. We must become comfortable with and appreciate other cultures. Speaking another language gives us not only an appreciation of another culture but also the ability to communicate with greater precision, even in our own language. The broader our vocabulary, the more choices we have in finding the best word. Even if we do not speak another language, we need at times to think from other cultural viewpoints if we are to work well together. Studying different belief systems, different values and rituals, makes us more flexible, more imaginative, and better at communicating.

Questions to ponder:

▶ Do you have colleagues from other cultures? What do you learn from them?

▶ Do you have customers from other cultures? How could you better meet their needs?

▶ Who are the leaders outside this country in your profession and industry?

▶ What books or periodicals from other cultures do you read?

▶ What advantages would there be in learning another language? Which one?

Use Information Technology

Although the cause-and-effect relationship is not yet clear, it is a fact that people who are computer literate earn 15 to 20 percent more than people who are not. It's also true that more and more jobs at all levels involve using computers—so learning to use the technology is no longer a matter of choice. In addition to the three R's, there is a C: Computing. Up-to-date technology connects us with the world. We can get information, chat with colleagues, and enlist new customers through online services and the Internet. Networked technology has leveled the playing field. We no longer need to go through the chain of command for information, services, or contacts. Working comfortably in this new technology is a prerequisite for future employability.

Are you up to date with information technology? Ask yourself the following questions:

▶ How have my computer skills helped me in the past month?

▶ Has a lack of computer skills limited my effectiveness? How?

▶ Whom do I know who could coach me to enhance my computer literacy?

▶ What information-handling tasks would I like to accomplish or learn in the next three months?

The mountain of software already available can make your life and work easier if you learn the basics. More powerful computers and software are coming. If you're not as much of a tech-head as you'd like to be, set some goals, enlist a coach (maybe even one of your children), and get to work.

Demonstrate Mastery

How can you let potential employers or customers know of your expertise, your value? There is only one way: through your accomplishments. You should have a portfolio that illustrates mastery of your profession or craft.

You must quantify in some way the value you can bring to your industry and organization.

Here's a good way to demonstrate your value to yourself and prepare to demonstrate it to others: conduct an annual accomplishment audit. The more you see the direct relationship between your work and its measurable benefits for organization and customers, the more secure you will feel. If you can't identify at least a few recent accomplishments, your value may be diminishing and your position may be precarious.

Think about these points:

► What have been your major accomplishments in the last six months?

► How have your accomplishments contributed to the bottom line? to better customer service? to new products? to the organization's reputation?

► How do others evaluate your accomplishments and skills?

► Who could help you sort this out?

Accomplishments that demonstrate your competencies are not limited to work, especially if you are a new worker. Look at all facets of your life— family, school, community, sports, politics, religion, the arts—for clues to your value and skill.

Initiate Work Projects

Few personal attributes are more valued than initiative. Employers and customers want motivated workers, people who see needs and take action to meet them. They know that self-starters are people of strength and passion who will enhance the workplace.

► Janet sees the need for a faster way to produce standard and customized workbook jackets. She develops a computer macro to do it, reducing the time required from two hours to fifteen minutes and producing a more attractive product in the bargain.

► Convinced that current warehouse procedures are highly inefficient, Manuel investigates which products are used most frequently and in what numbers and totally redesigns the work flow. This initiative saves him several hours of work each day, boosts company productivity, and builds his reputation in the company.

Perhaps you are driven by your passion and propose to come up with new ways to satisfy the needs of customers, clients, students, and others. Or perhaps you see limitations in yourself, areas where you have not yet achieved personal mastery. Whether your stimulus is internal or external, by initiating projects you build a reputation as a motivated worker whose services are to be coveted.

In these days when everyone is overworked, what makes you a committed worker? You audit projects to increase efficiency; you devise new ways to satisfy customers; you invent shortcuts to supply better products or services; and you do it all without being asked.

As a worker who wishes to act with initiative, ask yourself the following:

► What complaints have I heard from customers that warrant new or different procedures?

► What ideas do I have for improving my work operation or customer service? What would it take to implement them? What benefits would accrue?

NEW WORKER

▶ *Use these indicators as ways to begin your professional development.*

▶ *Talk with your friends, colleagues, or mentors about ways to make these behaviors a reality.*

▶ *Find organizations and jobs that reward and foster these behaviors.*

IN TRANSITION

▶ *Assess yourself against these indicators.*

▶ *Choose new work situations, organizations, and jobs that value these individual indicators and support you in bringing them into your own portfolio.*

EXPERIENCED WORKER

▶ *If you've been successful to date, it's likely you've already built your work life around most of these indicators. Emphasize their value when you're considering a different work situation.*

▶ *If you haven't accomplished your goals, adopt the indicators that will bring the biggest payouts. Be sure employers and business partners are aware of the benefits you bring them. Highlight your strengths!*

▶ What bottlenecks do I see in my current operations? How could I alleviate them?

▶ What learning project could I undertake that would both enhance my professional competencies and improve customer service?

Work Closely with Customers

There are a few highly self-directed, self-critical people who can work well in isolation. Most of us, however, derive pleasure and motivation from daily contact with colleagues or customers. The closer these links and the more frequent the feedback on how well you are doing, the more likely you are to find creative solutions to problems. One of the most valuable products of total quality improvement and reengineering is more direct access to and frequent communication with customers. As we eliminate levels of hierarchy and create cross-functional teams, each worker comes more directly in contact with customers.

Consider the following points:

▶ Who are your customers?

▶ How do your customers measure your effectiveness?

▶ How do you get feedback? How could you get it more frequently?

▶ What new products or services would help your customers?

▶ How would having more direct contact with customers benefit you?

Within the larger Web of Work, you weave your own life's work. The more unique and connected to real human needs it is, the more stable; the more in line with your passion and purpose, the higher its value to you and to others. These principles can guide your quest for a rewarding way of contributing to your community, your nation, and the world.

PART III

Professions

"Amateurs hope. Professionals work."

—*Elbert Hubbard*

*T*he secret to realizing your work potential and value to employers, colleagues, and customers is to become a master in a profession. In my work I ignore the conventional distinction between professions, trades, and crafts—and it is a distinction worth losing. Traditionally, a profession is considered a discrete discipline requiring a body of knowledge of some department of learning or science; a trade is an occupation requiring skilled manual or mechanical work. The distinction has been made on the basis of formal or "higher" education, as opposed to trade school or apprenticeship education. For succinctness, I will use the term "profession" to mean trades and crafts as well.

Every profession has a body of knowledge, specific practices, tools, and competency requirements, as well as acknowledged experts and leaders. Whatever your calling, your goal should be to become a master in your field—an acknowledged expert and leader. The importance of choosing and mastering a profession is the focus of the next three chapters. Chapter 5 will help you choose or focus on your profession; chapter 6 will explore the importance of professional mastery; and chapter 7 will help you examine the viability of your profession and implications for your long-term employability.

NEW WORKER

▶ If you are not working yet, choose a profession that you are passionate about, that supports your unique talents and purpose. If you can't decide, seek internships, volunteer work, or any other experience that will help you decide.

▶ Choosing a profession is crucial for long-term employability. If you are working, you are already situated in some profession. You can begin learning more about it, choosing a satisfying setting and mentor, or reevaluating your career choices.

IN TRANSITION

▶ You may be in transition because the niche in which you've been working doesn't "fit" you. In which professions have you already worked? Which professions appeal to you? Which professions give you a feeling of accomplishment? Which professions match your talents and purpose?

▶ If you already excel in a profession that is no longer needed in your company or industry, look for other organizations or industries that can use your special talents.

EXPERIENCED WORKER

▶ You may have worked for years and moved from job to job but never really excelled in a profession. If so, now's the time to pursue mastery aggressively.

▶ If you have excelled in a profession that is no longer required in your industry, look at other industries.

▶ If you have a longtime dream that requires you to learn another profession, take heart—having mastered one profession makes it easier for you to learn another.

Your Profession: A Stabilizing Choice

WHY DOES CHOOSING A PROFESSION stabilize your work life? Because professions are the most dependable, most enduring part of the Web of Work. Thinking in terms of a job rather than a profession is a common mistake, but short-sighted. A job is a small piece of a profession—a task you can do adequately without knowing its place in the overall scheme of things (such as processing a loan, or assembling direct mail). In a job, you are replaceable—just a cog in the machine. With a profession, however, you are part of a long tradition of specialization, a broad weave of interconnected disciplines.

Professions have evolved in response to human needs. We are social beings; we work to benefit others and to receive benefits in return. This tradeoff works best when everyone does the work he or she is best suited for and excels at. Because human needs do not disappear, professions are permanent, though evolving, features of the Web of Work.

Below are some examples of basic human needs and how professions have evolved to meet them.

Health.   Tribal specialists gathered herbs and other substances for their healing and restorative properties. Among their successors are today's physicians, pharmacologists, holistic medicine practitioners, botanists, chemists, biologists, homeopaths, geneticists, and others.

Home / shelter.   Beginning long before the dawn of history, people have constructed shelters for everyday living, worship, and tribal gatherings. Today the need for shelter is addressed by many different professions: architecture, civil engineering, urban planning, ergonomics, carpentry, electrical engineering, plumbing, landscaping, to name a few.

Leisure.   Archaeological and historical records show the evolution of leisure specialists from tribal storytellers and dancers through early minstrels, poets, and artists to the present broad array of media professionals such as writers, comedians, filmmakers, and rock stars.

All our professions can be linked to one or more of the basic human needs. New methods, technologies, and practices continue to evolve as we merge breakthroughs from other professions into our own. It's easy to see that if the basic patterns of thousands of years continue, as we have every reason to expect, they will remain the stable foundation on which to build your career and your contribution to your family and the community.

One Profession, Many Needs

Just like our civilization, professions have become more complex and versatile. Thus, if you are an airline pilot, you are instrumental in addressing many human needs: transportation, of course, but also work, social relationships, leisure, health, family, and economic security. You can make similar connections with other modern professions. Even more traditional professionals may find themselves serving other causes. Farmers who maintain wetlands are serving the needs of the environment for all of us; ranchers may devote part or all of their time to leisure by establishing guest ranches.

The more human needs your profession addresses, the more stable, portable, and versatile it will be—and the more industries and organizations you can practice it in. For instance, as an educator you could teach high school math, head a community college, deliver corporate training workshops, create computer-based instructional materials, or teach English as a second language for a multinational organization. Some professions, such as accounting, are found in virtually every kind of organization and industry.

If you live as fast-paced a life as most of us, it's easy to lose sight of what you are trying to do—the things you were so passionate about a few years back. Both to refocus on your mission and to evaluate your contribution to your community, it is helpful to think about how your profession is linked to the human condition.

Study the two lists in the sidebar on page 91. Link each human need on the left with as many professions on the right as you can that relate to it— even tenuously. Some professions are related to a multitude of basic human needs; see how many needs you can link each profession with. Add any professions you can think of that link to one or more needs.

The more clearly we see the benefit of professional expertise on the health of the community, the more motivated and caring we become.

Choosing a Profession: An Overview

How you intend to make a living and contribute to your community is one of the most important adult decisions you can make. Although some professions are easier to enter and learn than others, it takes ten years or more to become a master in any profession. Some require extensive education; most involve certain tools, practices, and competencies that take time to accumulate.

Your basic interests, personality, unique talents, and values predispose you toward certain professions. Your family history or community might pull you toward specific industries or organizations. Each industry or organization requires certain professions to achieve its mission. Although someone can give you a job, no one can give you a profession.

Can Your Profession Choose You?

Some of us spend much of our lives in search of a profession. Others start out blindly but before long, by chance, find something they are good at and for which they develop a zest and passion. And there are a fortunate few who know from an early age what they want to do with their life.

My nephew Joey felt his calling early. He drew houses when he was three; he won drawing and design contests in grade school and high school. He finished architecture school when the construction industry was in a slump. He worked construction for two years, learning some of the basics that would contribute to his profession. While pondering whether to use his skills in the Peace Corps or move back home to the Northeast, he got a break: an architectural firm hired him.

Joey is happy following his dream. Not everyone is so fortunate. If you are not clear about what you want to do, how you want to contribute and make a living, take stock of what you know about yourself. What do you do best? What comes naturally to you? You will be happiest if you choose a profession that fulfills the following:

► Harnesses your unique talents

► Fits your personality

► Lets you associate with people you like and respect

► Is valued in industries and organizations that are growing

► Requires continuous learning

► Lets you contribute directly to others

The closer your profession is to satisfying a specific human need and the closer you are to customers, the more fulfilled you will be. There will be a natural desire to assess the quality of your contribution in terms of your own satisfaction and that of others:

► Is the deck beautiful and functional?

Matching Needs

Human Need	Profession
Home / Shelter	Accountant
	Animal trainer
Family / Kinship	Architect
	Auto mechanic
Work / Career	Biologist
	Cosmetician
Social Relationships	Engineer
	Home nurse
Health—Physical and Mental	Interior designer
	Landscaper
Financial Security	Musician
	Occupational therapist
Learning	Painter
	Photographer
	Pilot
Transportation / Mobility	Salesperson
	Sanitation worker
Environment / Safety	Sculptor
	Social worker
Community	Software designer
	Teacher
	Tree surgeon
Leisure	TV producer
	Veterinarian
Spirituality	Writer

▶ Was the root canal painless?

▶ Do the colors of your living room convey the feeling you wanted?

▶ Is the fit of the joint perfect, letting no air or chemicals escape?

▶ Is the ad compelling?

Career Assessment: Where Are You Now?

Take a few minutes to assess where you are. Perhaps you have worked in a job for some time without having chosen a profession. You think of your work as a position rather than a profession. You know something about a profession but haven't thought in terms of mastering it. You haven't sought out experts, found a mentor, considered what you need to learn next, or taken the courses you need for the necessary background knowledge in the profession.

The tradition of equating salary with position rather than mastery has kept many workers from staying with a profession long enough to master it. If you're like many people, you may have been quite good in a technical specialty, but one day were promoted to management. Guess what? That's a new profession, with a whole new body of knowledge and practices required for excellence. Suddenly you are expected to know how to manage and motivate people, organize a department, and possibly maneuver in new political circles. The price you pay for your promotion may be lower competence, lack of confidence, and an increased risk of being "downsized"!

It's important to know where you are in your progress toward professional mastery. Read each of the following descriptions and check the ones that best fit your current situation. Then consider the questions and the suggested actions beneath each description you marked.

☐ ***Choosing a profession.*** I've been doing jobs but haven't yet thought in terms of a profession or a career.

▶ Review your job history. In which professions have you worked? Were some more fulfilling than others?

▶ Ask several people who know you well what profession they see you working in for the future.

▶ When you look at the list of human needs (p. 32), which ones appeal to you?

▶ What would your ideal work be? What profession is it in?

▶ Scan magazines and want ads to broaden your knowledge of various professions.

☐ ***Choosing between professions.*** I have held jobs and been interested in more than one profession but have not yet chosen the one in which I want to excel.

▶ Reflect on your most satisfying jobs. Which profession or professions were they in?

▶ Reflect on your major work accomplishments to date. In which profession do they fit?

▶ Look at the style and personality of people in the different professions in which you've worked. Do you identify more with one style or setting than another?

▶ Which basic human needs seem most compelling to you? What professions do they suggest (see p. 91)?

▶ Which profession do you see yourself in ten years from now?

☐ ***Positioning yourself in a profession.***   I have chosen a profession in which I want to excel and build mastery.

▶ Are you already working in an organization that excels in your profession? Which other organizations interest you?

▶ Can you identify eight or ten masters in your profession? If not, talk with colleagues, do some research, and find out who they are.

▶ Do you have a mentor? If not, whom could you ask to be your mentor?

▶ What are the six or eight major trends in your profession? What are their implications for your future?

▶ Have you joined associations in your profession?

☐ ***Excelling in your profession.***   I have chosen a profession and learned its basics. I am in an organization and an industry that need my professional savvy. I have a mentor.

▶ Who are the "best of the best" in your profession?

▶ Do you have opportunities to work with masters in your profession? If not, how could you make that happen?

▶ Do you spend time with your professional colleagues discussing problems, new technologies, or new ways of enhancing competencies?

▶ Have you structured projects, shows, experiments, or research that lets you work at the frontiers of your profession?

▶ Do you read the professional papers of the masters or study their work?

☐ ***Choosing between employment and entrepreneurship.*** I am an acknowledged master in my profession. I now need to assess which setting will let me learn and contribute the most, as well as fit my changing values and needs.

▶ Talk with colleagues who are self-employed and see what it takes to make that happen.

▶ Review your top ten values for the next five to ten years and decide which avenue is more in keeping with them. Discuss it with your spouse, family, and close friends.

▶ Interview five colleagues who are entrepreneurs and get a list of the pros and cons of this approach.

▶ Evaluate your financial needs and see how many different ways you could meet those needs.

▶ Consider the following:

Starting your own practice

Hooking up with a colleague who has become an entrepreneur

Finding a temporary agency that might broker your professional services

Moonlighting to see what it's like to be an entrepreneur

Telecommuting

Decide where you are on the path to mastery. When you have a good grasp of where you stand, what you need to do next will become evident. Mastering a profession will give you confidence and make it much easier for you to be running your career.

Mastery: Your Big Career Advantage

C HOOSING A PROFESSION connects you with the Web of Work in a way that holding a job doesn't. You can see directly how you are contributing to the care or satisfaction of others' needs. Being a part of a bigger system gives you confidence and stability. You can see how changes in other fields, industries, and organizations affect your career. You can adjust your career goals to take advantage of trends in any part of the system. But being a professional is not a passive state. One reason, perhaps the main reason, for focusing your attention on a profession is to become as good as you can be in your field—to be a master.

What Is a Master?

To have achieved mastery is to have "competency and artistry embedded in skillful practice"[1] and a "sense of proficiency, achievement, and autonomy in a selected profession or field of endeavor."[2] A more rigorous definition developed by my colleague Peter Hartwick and myself is "mastery of a profession is in the subtle, systematic integration of the biological, rational, and emotional aspects of the basic principles and practices of the craft."

We equate expert skill and knowledge with mastery. People who are masters in a profession are able to improvise, make new connections, test, experiment, and invent new strategies and approaches when the old ones aren't working. They can carry on their trade or profession independently, with no supervision. Masters have experienced so many variations of what works, what doesn't, and what can go wrong that they are rarely surprised or baffled by the unusual. They seem to know instinctively what to do, whom to call, where to look, and how to handle a crisis.

We all know what it feels like to be in the presence of a master. We are awed, humbled, and inspired in the same moment. Masters are our everyday heroes. Asked to list masters in various professions, most people will come up with a list much like the one shown on page 99. These people are recognized masters—the "sung" heroes, so to speak. For every master who is famous, however, thousands work in relative anonymity in schools, businesses, and public agencies, appreciated mostly by friends, family, colleagues, and other professionals.

Mastery Is the Foundation for Career Stability

Since you are reading this book, you want to compete for the kind of work you like to do—work that engages your passion, contributes to your community, and rewards your efforts. You will find that you have many competitors trying to get the same work. Developing depth and breadth in a profession, and the discipline that goes with it, is essential to your long-term success and your ability to respond quickly and intelligently to changes in the Web of Work.

Mastery Enhances Your Life

Virtue is its own reward. An athlete undertakes physical training to compete in contests of strength, endurance, and skill—but reaps the additional benefits of an attractive physique, physical grace, good health, and longevity. In the same way, training to become a master not only helps you compete for work but also conditions your mind, making it easier for you to learn. Once you have mastered the subtle distinctions, practices, and tools of one profession, you can more easily add a subdiscipline or even switch professions.

By becoming a master in pursuit of your passion, you avoid the atrophy of brain function that is known to plague those who focus on one small area in their work. You become more versatile, resilient, and able to solve complex problems. You gain an appreciation of excellence in other fields—including art, music, and literature—because you more readily recognize the high quality that results from mastery. Not least, your competence contributes to your sense of health and security.

Accomplished Masters

Fashion	**Liz Claiborne, Ralph Lauren**
Baseball	**Cal Ripken, Jr., Babe Ruth**
Architecture	**I.M. Pei, Frank Lloyd Wright**
Technology	**Steve Jobs, Bill Gates**
Social work	**Mother Teresa**
Physics	**Stephen Hawking**
Military science	**Norman Schwartzkopf**
Music	**Isaac Stern, Itzhak Perlman**
Hospitality	**Bill Marriott, Martha Stewart**
Cooking	**Julia Child, Paul Prudhomme**
Broadcasting	**Ted Turner**
Finance	**Peter Lynch, Warren Buffett**
Painting	**Matisse, Georgia O'Keeffe**

Mastery Builds Confidence

Confidence comes from feeling that you are in control of your life. It is a feeling that you begin building when you are young. As a child, you began that first frightening, unsteady ride on your new bicycle. After a few false starts, you got the hang of it. You learned that you turn by leaning; you began to feel that as long as you kept moving you weren't going to fall over. With competence came the confidence to ride all the way to school and back. Eventually, you embarked on long trips or braved those intimidating mountain trails with self-assurance.

Maria Montessori founded a school and developed an educational philosophy based on the principle of mastery. She put children of differing ages in the same room to work together, learn from, and coach one another. They learned to grow tulips, count with objects, read stories, clean tables, and help one another with daily tasks. They became masters of their environment. Their sense of accomplishment at mastering ever more complex tasks gave them a pride and confidence that showed.

Being good at something is an instinctive need in all of us. It is part of having control of our environment, of taking charge of our life. The longer it takes to find a profession and become accomplished in it, the lower is our self-esteem and confidence. The loss is not only ours but our community's. Lacking skills, the weakest among us may turn to addiction, dependency, or crime.

Companies *Need* Masters

Becoming a master in your profession makes you more valuable to organizations that need your skills. You can sell yourself to companies as easily as you could a product or service. Not only are your skills more evidently valuable, but with your greater confidence you can present youself more persuasively.

You don't really have to sell companies on the advantages of using masters, however. Most are already well aware of the benefits. As organizations have become smaller, flatter, and faster, their need for talented experts has increased rapidly. Autonomous work teams need masters they can turn to quickly for guidance and expertise. Trusting complex problems and critical strategic decisions to anyone but an experienced master can produce shattering results.

Small Mistakes Make Big Trouble

Let's take a ridiculously obvious example. Imagine you are on an airplane at 37,000 feet, at night, getting tossed around in a violent storm. Whom of the following would you want at the controls?

▶ A pilot with the minimum hours required to fly the plane and who has passed all the written and simulator tests and met the minimum requirements for a license?

▶ A pilot with the same license but who has flown in all conditions for twenty years, instructed other pilots, and helped design the training program?

We would all readily agree that the second pilot's experience, knowledge, and ability to handle routine tasks automatically while dealing with complex and dangerous situations could easily make the difference between catastrophe and survival.

Of course, few situations in any job, industry, or company carry this kind of immediate life-or-death risk. This can lead to complacency. Careless managers may put unqualified people in situations where they cause missteps or accidents. Only after the damage has been done do we recognize that poor decisions in these arenas can have severe repercussions:

▶ An inexperienced lathe operator turns out machine parts a few micrometers too small, resulting in the delivery to a major customer of a batch of defective valves.

► A customer relations representative who is a marginal reader is reluctant to look up parts numbers for certain customers, causing them to drift to competitors over a period of months.

As you can see, there's a lot more at stake in these situations than meets the eye. It doesn't take a major crash to finish off a business.

Masters Make Natural Leaders

Most people would think that the person most likely to be a successful business leader would be someone who had all the attributes we associate with a master. Who else should lead but someone with competence, confidence, creativity, passion, and a willingness to try new ideas? And yet, surprising as it may seem, a lot of recent talk would have it that we need fewer specialists and more generalists. Indeed, many organizations have people in key positions who are said to be "good generalists," which is often code for managers with experience in a variety of business settings and mastery in none.

There are many examples of organizations that don't have the leadership depth to grapple with complex, serious problems, where the person at the helm has little real-life experience in any of the industry's core professions. A highly intelligent marketing professional might become an outstanding leader of an advertising firm but, without the proper technical mastery, would probably be ineffective heading a major telecommunications company.

Specialists Are Good Learners

Companies know that masters are valuable, adaptable resources. People who have invested the time and developed the discipline to become expert in a specialty can deal with a wide range of tasks and problems outside their specialty. There are two outstanding factors behind this phenomenon. First, the deep learning involved in mastering a specialty enriches and enhances your synaptic pathways in ways that make the brain a better learning machine. This increased learning capacity can then be brought to bear on other problems and tasks.

In addition, many seemingly unrelated problems and principles have much more in common than we might think. The brain is, among other things, a marvelous pattern-recognition device. The patterns learned in mastering a specialty give the master special insight into similar patterns in other disciplines. An expert in hydrology, for instance, is more likely than most to see certain important similarities between the movement of groundwater through layers of limestone and the movement of electrons through the silicon layers of a semiconductor.

> ### STEPS TO MASTERY
>
> **1. Unconscious Incompetence
> (apprentice)**
>
> **2. Conscious Incompetence
> (technician)**
>
> **3. Conscious Competence
> (mentor/coach)**
>
> **4. Unconscious Competence
> (master/leader)**

The Road to Mastery

What does it take to become a master? *Ten to seventeen years of practice,* among other things, according to a study conducted by Dr. Benjamin Bloom of Northwestern University.[3] The process can't be rushed. The generalist often touted as the solution to America's corporate problems thinks nothing of moving through three professions—marketing to finance to management, for instance—in a decade or less. This pattern is often set in graduate school, where knowledge without practice can get you a master's degree, but not mastery.

One way of looking at mastery is as a process involving awareness and competence. Every beginner starts out, naturally, in a condition of ignorance and incompetence. At first, the person isn't even aware of this lack of competence because she doesn't know what there is to learn (unconscious incompetence). First, she must become conscious of how much work needs to be done, how much there is to learn, and how little of it she knows or can do (conscious incompetence). Years of disciplined study and practice lead to a state of conscious competence in which the learner is fully aware of her actions—that is, they do not come automatically. In the final phase (unconscious competence), the learner is highly competent and knowledgeable in her field and can accomplish most tasks automatically, almost instinctively.

This final stage is one definition of mastery: unconscious competence. We see examples of unconscious competence around us every day:

► A pilot makes a slight control input while simultaneously talking on the radio, looking at a chart, and remembering the next radio frequency.

► A seamstress feeds the delicate silk effortlessly through the sewing machine, turning out a flawless sleeve while talking with a colleague.

► With a few dabs of a brush, a painter mixes several colors that evoke the shadow of a cloud on the surface of a stormy sea.

Being in the presence of such mastery can be exhilarating. It's even more exhilarating when the skill is one we understand. The most appreciative (and critical) audience for any master is other masters.

Start Early

Choosing a profession early in life focuses energy and attention when they are at their most abundant. If you are twenty when you begin your quest for mastery, and if you are diligent and steadfast in that quest, you may be recognized by your peers as an accomplished expert by the time you are thirty or thirty-five.

An early start is especially important in developing manual or language skills. But it's never too late to start. In fact, it can be argued that mastery of any profession comes more easily after a person has mastered certain life and coping skills, such as committing to a cause, maintaining focus, postponing gratification, and other skills often lumped under the term "self-discipline."

Learn the Competencies

Every profession has a required set of competencies—clusters of related skills required for mastery. Although skills may change considerably over the lifetime of one professional, many of the competencies stay the same. Consider the competencies required to be an accomplished salesperson:

► Presentation know-how

► Product knowledge

► Communication skills (listening)

► Industry knowledge

► Planning and scheduling expertise

► Negotiation skills

In workshops, I often ask, "Who was the first salesperson?" If no one guesses it, I can usually make the case that Eve was the first to use these sales competencies, including product knowledge (properties and benefits of the apple) and planning the best schedule for communicating and negotiating with Adam, her customer. Sales competencies haven't changed a lot over the centuries.

> **THE MASTER**
>
> ► *has depth, skill, knowledge, and expertise in a profession*
>
> ► *produces results that are of value to others*
>
> ► *is known by and has worked with experts*
>
> ► *is unconsciously competent*
>
> ► *is sought after by other professionals for his or her wisdom*

Study with a Master

Once you are confident that you have focused on the right set of competencies, you are well on your way to developing the essential skills of your profession. But which competencies do you need to learn first, and how can you learn them? These are questions supervisors used to answer. Now, however, there are fewer supervisors to ask, and you may be the only person in your profession on the team.

This is where the guidance of a master in your profession can get you focused on the right questions and activities and speed up your learning. Some professions are learned in academic settings (law, architecture, medicine, engineering, and so on); others are learned through apprenticeships. Find a mentor you are comfortable with, someone whose mastery you and others respect and whose professional focus coincides with or approximates your own.

Practice, Practice, Practice

In mastering your profession, you will have access to information, expert advice, and other resources, all of which are essential to mastery. Mentors, colleagues, associations, and journals will help you assess and determine the changing skills and competencies required for success. But no matter what resources are available to you, there is no substitute for the self-imposed

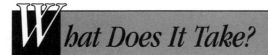
What Does It Take?

If you want to be a master in your profession, look at the whole picture:

▶ *What practices must you master in the progression from apprentice to technical contributor to professional to master?*

▶ *What experiences must you have to be able to practice the basics and acquire the discipline of the profession?*

▶ *What knowledge and principles must you acquire?*

▶ *What texts or books must you read?*

▶ *Who are the leaders in the profession, and what do they say are the essential competencies?*

rigor of study, practice, error, and correction, over and over, in your never-ending quest for excellence.

Every profession has its own routine work requirements. To master a skill, you have to work with the tools of the trade for many years.

▶ A master cabinetmaker has to know all the varieties of wood available in order to choose the right one for each job.

▶ The master painter has to have experienced every shade of blue in order to know the exact color for the sky of a particular place, weather, and time of day.

▶ A master technician has to have fixed hundreds of security systems in order to troubleshoot one in several minutes, repair it, and move on to the next.

Identifying each of the dozens of competencies or skills of your profession is only the beginning. You must practice, practice, practice so that each one becomes deeply ingrained in your body. You will become unconsciously competent. Mother Nature cannot be fooled. The mind and body function and learn on their own terms. The path to mastery is profoundly indifferent to faddish shortcuts, however well intentioned or attractive they might be. Only intense practice produces mastery.

Do the Dirty Work

One big reason more people don't become masters in their profession is that the road to mastery is often unpleasant. It leads you through years and years of work that may be difficult, unglamorous, and routine before you get recognition. If you want to make movies, you'd better learn to load film, check sound systems, set lights, shovel sand on an artificial beach, negotiate a labor contract, and deal with temperamental actors—because even if you don't end up doing these jobs as a master, you must be able to judge how well others are doing them for you.

The most serious issue with newcomers entering a profession is the attitude that, as professionals, they don't have to take orders, work hard, or do the grunt work—that's for laborers, wage earners, and nonprofessionals. Those who never learn why a master has to be familiar with these tasks are unlikely ever to become masters.

One of my favorite movies illustrates this point well. In *The Karate Kid,* a boy wants a karate master to teach him to defend himself against school-yard bullies. The master first gives the boy a long series of menial tasks: painting a fence, polishing a car. The boy objects—he wants to fight, not shine the master's car. The master is not swayed; he sternly keeps the boy doing menial work. Finally, when the boy is able to perform without conscious thought the up-and-down strokes of painting, the smooth circular motions of waxing, and countless other simple motions, the master shows him how to put them all together in the complex practice of karate. The discipline of the art, the boy learns, requires the intense but unconscious coordination of the mind, the body, and the emotions under less-than-ideal conditions. It cannot be rushed.

Demonstrate Results

You have achieved mastery when you can demonstrate excellent results, whether in the construction of a house, the preparation of a meal, the performance of a piano sonata, or the rearing of a child. Indeed, the quality of the result may be your only clue that you have truly become a master. You may arrive at this achievement unaware. Seasoned professionals develop instincts and habits that produce useful and desired results. But when asked why or how they did what they do, they often have to stop and think before being able to answer. They have moved from deliberate, conscious application of effort to unconscious competence, which usually is reflected in a comment like "Well, I don't know. I just do it that way."

NEW WORKER

▶ *If you are already working in your chosen profession, focus not only on your job but on your profession as well.*

▶ *Find a mentor who can help you answer the questions posed in this chapter. Ask that person to guide you and keep you focused on mastery.*

▶ *If you haven't chosen a profession, make that your quest now.*

▶ *Use the work you are doing now to develop your basic work attitudes and human competencies—working as a team member, listening, questioning, communicating, computer literacy, and language skills.*

IN TRANSITION

▶ *If you haven't chosen a profession, now's the time. Use your current situation as a powerful platform for tackling the question of profession.*

▶ *Get clear on why you are in your current transition. Are you unhappy in your current profession? Have you never chosen a profession but simply done whatever work came your way? Is it because you've never had a great mentor, or enough time or commitment?*

▶ *Decide what stage you are in—apprentice, technician, mentor/coach, or master.*

▶ *Ask three or four masters in the profession to give you their honest assessment of your competencies.*

EXPERIENCED WORKER

▶ *Evaluate your level of mastery. Are you at the apprentice, technician, mentor/coach, or master level?*

▶ *Ask masters in your profession to evaluate your work. Does their assessment agree with yours? Do you need a bigger playground for challenge and learning?*

▶ *Examine your current situation. Do you need to be working with others like yourself? Should you broaden your experience by working for other organizations as a contract or temporary worker?*

▶ *This is a time in your life to excel. Do you have unfulfilled dreams? Consider a move into that second or third profession to make the contribution you want to make. Go for it!*

The Power of Professional Mastery

Being a master means being a leader in your profession. You are on the cutting edge, always learning, always alert for new ideas, for better ways of doing things. Whatever happens in the Web of Work that affects your profession, your industry, and your organization, you are the person who adapts the work to it, and who sets the standard for the industry and your colleagues. You are in the position of adapting not only your own career to changing conditions but the careers of other professionals as well.

Professions evolve continually. The basic competencies change little from year to year, but the skills and techniques often make quantum leaps overnight. The invention of new technologies such as lasers, computers, and artificial earth satellites bring enormous changes in all industries. Surgeons still learn anatomy, but sutures have given way to endoscopy and laparoscopy. International financiers still study world supply and demand, but transoceanic cables rust away beneath gleaming Telstars. Professionals adapt to new ways of satisfying the essential human needs, masters show them the way.

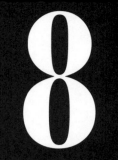

Your Profession's Vitality

WHETHER WE ARE CONSCIOUS OF IT or not, jobs, organizations, industries, and professions are in continuous flux. The Web of Work responds to changes in any of its parts. Workers unaware of changes outside their sphere are often surprised to find themselves among the discarded pieces of the old economic order. Working hard at their jobs, they fail to see that a new technology is eliminating the need for their skills. Accomplished professionals find themselves out in the cold after their organization's mission changes and their profession is no longer required.

The following indicators are designed to reveal where your profession fits in the entire Web of Work. Taken together, they will help you detect trends and prepare yourself for them. Given fair warning, you can stay ahead of changes by improving your professional standing, learning new skills and competencies, or searching out new opportunities elsewhere.

Your Profession's Importance to the Organization

Does your current organization need people from your profession to achieve its mission? There are several ways to find out:

EIGHT INDICATORS OF PROFESSION VITALITY

1. **Essential to the purpose of the organization**

2. **Transfers to other industries and organizations**

3. **Competencies apply to other professions**

4. **Provides financial and personal compensation**

5. **Professional associations exist**

6. **Obvious path to mastery**

7. **Age-independent**

8. **Requires communication outside the organization**

▶ Review the organization's mission and strategies carefully to determine the relevance of your profession. Get a copy of the business plan and department objectives. The more your profession is needed to provide products or services to customers, the less at risk you are.

▶ Ask people who know the organization well to name the top four or five professions required for achieving its mission and strategies. See whether your profession is included.

NEW WORKER

► *Use the indicators as aids in choosing a powerful profession and finding organizations and industries that need your skill.*

► *Seek mentoring, experience, and learning opportunities.*

► *Find others in your chosen profession with whom you can share ideas and opportunities.*

► *Don't be so worried about finding a job that you are tempted to choose a place that won't serve you in the long term.*

IN TRANSITION

► *Use these indicators to interview potential employers.*

► *Don't leave one bad situation for another. If you're not progressing at one company or position, choose carefully before making a move.*

► *Get advice from others you trust who know the situation you've left.*

► *Don't be in such a hurry to find a job that you repeat past mistakes.*

EXPERIENCED WORKER

► *If you're working, assess future options in your current organization.*

► *Find other industries and organizations that fit these indicators.*

► *Do a search to see where else you might work, what value you could add, and how best to sell yourself.*

► *See how many different ideal work situations you can create for yourself, then choose the one that makes you the happiest. If you're a master, the sky's the limit.*

► Read public-relations statements as well as selection and recruiting information to see if people in your profession are highlighted in organization communications.

► Review any downsizing or reengineering information to see if jobs in your profession are being eliminated.

▶ Find out what professional-development support, such as tuition aid, advanced degrees, apprenticeship programs, mentoring, professional conferences, development experiences, and high-visibility projects, is available to people in your profession.

These inquiries will give you a strong sense of the importance of your profession in your organization. If you find that your talents are required, continue to build your visibility in the organization and your professional reputation in the industry. If not, start researching other organizations or industries.

Is Your Profession Transferable?

This is a very important issue relating to your long-term employability. In some sense, the more industries and organizations that need your professional acumen, the more options you have. Some professions are restricted to a few industries, so that when the industry is at risk, the profession is also in trouble. For several decades, aerospace engineers were in high demand in just two industries: defense and commercial aviation. Airline deregulation and the end of the Cold War forced both industries into a major retrenchment. These industries moved from growth to decline and fewer aerospace engineers were required. If your profession is not readily transferable, you should be especially alert to economic, political, social, and technological trends affecting your industry and organization.

There are several ways to check out your employability in other industries and organizations:

▶ Study the Sunday classifieds in prominent newspapers for four consecutive weeks and list all the organizations and industries that want people in your profession.

▶ Ask six savvy people to name the industries that most need your professional services.

▶ Ask six people in your profession for a list of industries and organizations that hire people with your professional talents. If possible, get names of specific projects or jobs.

Keep asking until you are fairly sure of just how many industries might need your professional expertise.

Are Your Competencies Transferable?

In every profession, you need certain competencies to be successful; others are desirable but not essential. It is important for you to know the difference, because certain competencies are required or valued in a variety of professions. If the need for your profession is phased out of an organization, the nonessentials in your old profession may turn out to be the essential competencies in another profession. You may be able to use the transferable competencies to move into another profession within the organization.

This is a good time to begin evaluating your professional value in terms of its transferability. Brainstorm as many jobs as you can that would profit from your competencies. See examples on page 117.

Financial Compensation

Justly or not, the value society attaches to our contribution is measured in monetary terms. Each profession has an upper and lower financial boundary. How much can you expect to be paid for your work? It depends on several factors:

▶ the amount of education or training required to master the profession

► the need for the competencies required by the profession

► the number of professionals in the market (the lower the number, the higher the pay)

► the income the professional generates for the company

► the sector of the economy (public versus private)

Study each of these variables and note their effects on the profession that you are interested in. See if you can think of other variables that might affect your compensation:

► Are there interesting new ways to market or package your professional talents to enhance your income potential? Explore this question with friends and colleagues.

► What are the traditional upper and lower compensation limits of your profession? Where can you get this information? Knowing this will help you ask for a market-value salary.

Professional Associations

One of the easiest and least expensive ways to enhance your professional standing and development is to join a professional association. Conferences, briefing sessions, problem solving with colleagues, brainstorming with master professionals, sharing new procedures, discussing new technologies—this is where learning happens. A good conference is like a jazz festival: you hear what the other bands are doing, sit in on jam sessions, meet the masters and the new talent, and find yourself coming up with new ideas that wouldn't have occurred to you deep in the recesses of your cave.

In times past, when the hunters returned with their kill or the farmers had harvested their crops, everyone sat around the fire or the dinner table to celebrate their good fortune and pass along the lessons learned. We need such rituals even today so that seasoned veterans can pass on their knowledge to members of the next generation and inspire them to take the actions needed to advance their profession. Take any opportunity you can find—conferences, dinners, informal mentoring sessions—to learn from the masters.

Answer the following questions:

▶ What are the important associations in my profession?

▶ When, where, and how do they meet?

Jobs Arise from Competencies

Competency	Profession	Job
People development	Counseling Management Education	Teacher
Economic forecasting	Economics Politics Strategic planning	Economic analyst
Software assessment	Education Accounting Management information systems Management	Technology manager
Spatial design	Interior design Architecture Graphic design Photography	Architect
Sales	Sales Public relations Hotel management Marketing	Marketing manager

▶ Which members of the association do I know?

▶ How do professionals in my area share new learning, issues, and problems?

▶ How active am I in the association? What more could I contribute?

Formal Mastery Path

Although all professions are, by definition, needed and useful, some are more difficult to master than others. To be a master painter, cabinetmaker, physicist, or investment manager takes more innate skill, more education, more experience, more mentoring, or a longer apprenticeship than do becoming a house painter, general carpenter, lab technician, or bank teller.

Many people have learned their profession without formal schooling, sometimes entirely on their own. In fields such as law and medicine, however, years of schooling are needed to acquire enough knowledge to begin. Professions that cost more and take longer to enter tend to be more financially rewarding.

Here are some mastery-path issues to think about:

▶ How long does it take, on average, to be seen as a master in your profession?

▶ What is the balance between school time and practice time required for excellence?

▶ Are the potential financial and spiritual rewards worth the time and energy it would take you to master the profession?

▶ Are masters in your profession highly respected, or do people feel that anyone could learn to do the work?

Age-Independence

Some professions are for the young. If your ambition is to be a master in competitive sports, modeling, dance, flight testing, or other fields where physical attractiveness, strength, agility, coordination, or endurance are paramount, expect to peak in your twenties or thirties. Other professions impose higher but stricter age limits; commercial pilots are required to retire at sixty, although this kind of limit is more often being challenged in court.

A few masters in these professions go into other fields closely related to their mastery. An athlete, for example, might enter coaching, sports medicine, or sports broadcasting. The wisest have a backup profession to turn to after age begins to diminish their physical assets. Most of these backups emphasize the mind—which continues to improve—over body. Many well-known sports figures have saved some of their celebrity salaries and invested in businesses. Some even take a hand in running these businesses and might tell you that the same strategic savvy that made them great on the playing field can prove useful in other competitive arenas.

Here are some age-related questions to consider when choosing a profession:

▶ How important are physical agility, skill, and stamina for excellence in the profession you're considering?

▶ Is there a ceiling for the length of time you can work in the profession?

▶ Is the profession geared more toward youth than experience?

▶ Are there any stated or unstated age limits in the profession?

Communicate Outside Your Organization

The more masters you have access to in your profession, the faster you will learn. Often, especially if you work in a small organization, this means talking with professionals in other organizations. This is your best source of new learning and for information about issues, problems, and developments in your profession. Some companies try to limit such outside communication to protect trade secrets. Whatever you can share and learn—short of jeopardizing your company's competitive position or running afoul of anti-trust laws—will help you become a master in your profession. Use every resource you can lay a hand on, from trade journals, on-line chat rooms, and informal networking to national and international conferences.

Another source of learning, one that should be considered essential, is feedback from customers, clients, or colleagues. You have to know how you are doing in the eyes of those who benefit from or are affected by your services. The more you hear from others about your performance quality, about what works and what doesn't, the faster you will acquire essential competencies and master your profession.

Questions to ponder:

► What associations or meetings do you attend that increase the opportunities for learning from colleagues in your profession?

► How and when could you create opportunities to observe people doing similar work in other companies?

► Can you use e-mail or the Internet to increase your communication with others in your profession?

► What tools and resources do you have for comparing your competencies to those of others in your profession working in other organizations?

Stay Current and Portable in Your Profession

Remember: *your profession is always evolving.* As new practices, technologies, and methods emerge, you must acquire new competencies and skills. Continuous learning is essential to maintaining your professional mastery. I highly recommend that you use the following research questions to keep yourself up to speed in your professional niche. Find others who are more experienced than you and talk with them about these questions.

> ► What are the core competencies required for mastery in my profession?

> ► How do I stack up with regard to the core competencies?

> ► Who are the experts or leaders in my profession?

> ► What projects, assignments, or work experiences would keep me at the forefront of your profession? How can I get one of them?

> ► What journals and periodicals capture the trends in my profession?

> ► What professional associations can keep me abreast of the leading-edge thinking in my profession?

Have these conversations frequently and you will stay ahead of the curve in your life's work. You will feel confident. Your contributions will stabilize your work and reputation.

PART IV

Industries

"All great change has come from outside the firm, not from inside."

—*Peter Drucker*

After professions, the most stable and enduring part of the Web of Work is its industries—groups of professions and organizations providing products and services for a common set of human needs, such as transportation, health, or finance. Industries appear, evolve, develop, stabilize, decline, and disappear or transform and move into another phase of growth. We've seen this recently with the automotive industry, telecommunications, and the energy industries.

You don't have to be a sociologist or a soothsayer to predict how trends will affect you. The shock waves of change that will eventually affect your work show up early as industry trends. The earlier you can spot a trend and foresee its ramifications—a change in your profession, a merger, the outsourc-

ing of your job, or the demise of your organization—the more time you have to prepare.

If you can spot trends when they begin to affect your industry, you still have plenty of time to react. You can tell which sectors are likely to grow and which sectors are about to be swept away or transformed, or whether the industry as a whole is growing, stable, or declining. This information is critical to your career planning; it allows you to identify the zones and niches of an industry that are best suited to your abilities and aspirations.

Part IV will help you become more industry savvy and position yourself in the Web of Work. You will learn

■ how to choose the right industry, given your profession

NEW WORKER

▶ Scan all your options before you commit to an industry or company.

▶ Using the eight indicators in chapter 10, assess the vitality of several industries that need your professional know-how. Which will enhance your professional development? What niches are being created?

IN TRANSITION

▶ Consider the pros and cons of staying in or leaving your current industry. Do industry trends indicate a continued need for your profession? Or are you in transition because your profession is becoming less essential?

▶ Examine whether your industry is growing, stable, or declining. What new niches have been created? Which old ones are closing? Avoid staying with or moving into industry sectors that are shrinking.

▶ If your professional functions were to be outsourced, investigate the industry where the function is now housed.

EXPERIENCED WORKER

▶ Ask yourself whether your profession is essential for your industry. Do you have experience in other industries that might offer new opportunities?

▶ Determine whether your industry is growing, stable, or declining. Think about what decisions you will have to make in each case.

■ *how to analyze the growth cycle of an industry and see its impact on your organization or job*

■ *the anatomy of industries—how they grow into important zones and niches*

■ *the importance of discovering industry trends and changes early in the game*

■ *eight reliable indicators of a viable industry*

Part IV will help you see and feel subtle vibrations in the industry web before they become major tremors. You'll learn to see options that others don't see. You will gain in anticipation, direction, confidence, and career stability.

Industries and Their Trends

*L*IKE THE WOMEN in the medical supply factory we discussed in chapter 3, most people take the existence of their job and their organization for granted. They may work most of their lives in a single industry and spend little time thinking about it or the trends that affect it. Then, when the inevitable changes occur, they are unprepared for the sudden loss of a job or for the merger or shutdown of their company.

One key to building a stable work life is to keep your eye on the bigger picture—the industry you are working in or planning to enter. Industries last longer, on the whole, than the organizations and jobs they contain. Every industry has a core set of continually evolving professions and competencies that outlast it and can be transferred from one industry to another. An industry exists to address one or more human need on a large scale. A company competes successfully by organizing the work of professionals to address those needs. To do so, it creates, changes, and eliminates jobs and fills those jobs with a constantly shifting group of workers.

There are two basic questions to ask yourself about your industry:

▶ Is my profession essential to the core mission of the industry?

▶ Is my industry growing, stable, or declining?

Knowing, or at least continually thinking about, the answers to these questions keeps you more in touch with the early warning signs of changes coming your way.

How Much Does Your Industry Need You?

Some professions cross industry boundaries. Accounting, sales, marketing, management, customer service, human resources, and administration, for example, play a role in the operations of almost every industry. But each is a core profession in some industries, a support profession in others. Examine the following list of industries.

Accounting is a core profession in the financial services industry, of course. Insurance companies, brokerage houses, tax preparation firms, compensation and benefits companies, and banks rely heavily on accountants to deliver their primary products and services. Outside the financial services and business services industries, however, accounting plays a secondary role. The automobile industry, for example, employs accountants, but

*I*ndustries

Advertising	**Energy**	**Petroleum refining**
Aerospace	**Entertainment**	**Pharmaceutical**
Apparel	**Financial Services**	**Photography**
Automobile	**Food and beverages**	**Publishing, printing**
Building materials	**Forest and paper products**	**Real estate**
Chemicals	**Furniture**	**Recreation, leisure**
Cleaning products	**Health care**	**Social services**
Computers, office equipment	**Hospitality, lodging**	**Telecommunications**
Construction	**Industrial and farm equipment**	**Textiles**
Cosmetics	**Legal services**	**Tobacco**
Defense	**Manufacturing**	**Toys**
Education	**Market research**	**Training and development**
Electronic equipment	**Motor vehicles and parts**	**Waste management**

mechanical engineers, industrial designers, and marketers are obviously more important to the business of manufacturing and selling cars. An accountant could make a good career in the car business but would probably find more career stability in insurance or banking.

Are *You* Essential?

When I ask workshop participants this question, the human resources, administration, finance, and public relations professionals usually go into shock. After they recover, however, they talk calmly and intelligently of the possibility that their expertise will be outsourced. Some consider changing industries. Others think they might like to freelance or do temporary work with several organizations in the same industry. We'll examine working freelance and temporary, along with other employment alternatives, in chapter 17. Still others resolve to secure their place in the organization by working harder. They are the ones who see the risk but have other concerns that hinder changing organizations.

When companies downsize and outsource functions, they usually do so in the growing awareness that some professions are no longer required within the industry. Unfortunately, many outplaced workers fail to understand this. They find new jobs in the same industry, setting themselves up for a repeat experience.

In the list of industries on page 129, which absolutely require your profession to accomplish their objectives? If you're new to the industry, check your assessments by consulting workers in the industry, reading trade magazines, and scanning annual reports. Choosing well is more important if your profession is not industry-specific, such as customer service or information technology. You can find work almost anywhere, but you're more likely to have a stable and rewarding career if you build your mastery in an industry that requires your expertise.

Are You First or Second String?

Knowing where your profession stands in your current industry and organization is essential in designing a sustainable career. "Primary" professions are those in which your expertise is absolutely required for the organization to accomplish its core mission. "Secondary" professions are those that are *not essential* to directly accomplishing that mission, but still important to the efficiency of the organization. Secondary functions might be better handled by outside firms specializing in, for example, human resources, marketing, or education. Hiring this expertise as consultants rather than in-house staff sometimes saves businesses money, and is often advantageous for the employees as well, since they will be surrounded by similar colleagues from whom they can learn. In modern times we have occasionally emphasized secondary over primary professions. The table on the next page, listing some primary and secondary professions in three industries, reveals this tendency.

Same profession (say, management), different industry—different importance. It makes all the difference whether you're essential to the mission of the industry or in a support role. If you were a leader in a company and had to decide where to spend money for talent development in your organization, which would you choose, the primary or the secondary professions? This is the reasoning going on as companies in many industries as they try to streamline. The trend is to outsource the secondary professions or to build alliances with firms that supply that expertise.

Think about the industry you are now working in or contemplating entering. Is your profession essential to the industry you work in, or does it mainly provide support services? If you are in a primary profession, you stand a better chance of building a long-term career in that industry. If not,

Assess Your Industry

Address these questions:

► **Which professions are most essential to your present industry?**

► **How would most people in your industry rate your current profession?**

► **Name three other industries (or niches within your current industry) in which your profession plays an essential role.**

► **Name three people you know in each of these other industries of whom you could ask the above questions. Schedule some time with each and see what you can learn.**

Primary and Secondary Professions

Industry	Primary Profession	Secondary Profession
Education	Teaching	Security
	Writing	Fund raising
	Counseling	Accounting
	Software design	Administration
Home construction	Carpentry	Interior design
	Plumbing	Marketing
	Electrical engineering	Security
	Painting	Accounting
Pharmacology	Chemistry	Administration
	Biology	Advertising
	Sales	Finance
	Product development	Public relations

it might be a good idea to start looking into other industries where your profession is found at the core rather than the margins.

People who can assess their industry prospects objectively, and who get other peoples' assessment, have a decided advantage in designing their future. If their profession is not essential to their current industry, they can begin taking action well before the organization they're working in decides to downsize or outsource that work.

Where Is Your Industry in Its Life Cycle?

Know the history of your current or prospective industry. Become familiar with its origins, its traditions, its practices.

- ▶ What needs did it arise to satisfy?

- ▶ Does the need still exist?

- ▶ How well did it adapt when conditions changed?

- ▶ Is it still adapting to changes?

- ▶ Is it essential in satisfying its original need?

- ▶ Is it growing, staying the same, or shrinking?

- ▶ How many boom-and-bust cycles has it been through?

- ▶ Is the number of professions involved increasing, stable, or declining?

- ▶ Are these professions becoming obsolete or staying ahead of the trends?

Questions like these will help you determine the likelihood of having a vital career if you stay in your industry.

The computer industry is an example of a young, booming, volatile industry. Twenty years ago, the action was in a few companies that made million-dollar mainframes and supercomputers. Within a few years, that segment of the industry was in decline because of low-cost microcomputers many people could afford. These new machines could do most of the work required in an ordinary office and rested comfortably on an ordinary desk. Industry powerhouses such as IBM, Digital, Control Data, and Cray lost their market dominance in a couple of decades. Large companies can rebound, of course, but it is often the small, innovative, start-up company that wins the competition with its flexibility and fighting spirit. As a whole, however, the entire computer industry is young and is expected to grow enormously over the next several decades.

As you study the history of other industries, you will see patterns:

▶ In the growth phase, many zones and niches emerge, both temporary and permanent, occupied by hundreds of organizations and millions of jobs, as in telecommunications and electronics today. Alliances, mergers, spin-offs, and buyouts occur frequently. The new technologies spurring this frenetic activity come mostly from outside the industry.

▶ When growth stabilizes, some zones disappear or shrink and are replaced by new ones. For example, in the garment industry, when the retail emphasis moved away from department stores to boutiques and super discount stores, the requirement for fashion designers, pattern markers, textile workers, yarn and dye technicians continued to exist. However, their work moved to different organizations, both at the high and low ends in the retail garment industry.

▶ Industries in decline are characterized by renewed intensity of closings, mergers, hostile takeovers, and downsizing as surviving companies fight over the remaining scraps of resources or shrinking markets. Industries currently struggling include the defense and lumber industries.

Keep an eye out for these signals in other organizations in your industry. Your organization or job may not be at the top of the list to indicate a major turn, but if you pay close attention to your colleagues and competitors, you can see what's coming before it happens to you. That's why observing the whole Web of Work is so important.

Catching Industry Trends

Industries can provide a broad environment in which to network, follow complex developments, learn about customer needs, and build new niches for taking care of people and their communities. Seeing and understanding work as webs of interrelated industries can go a long way toward reducing your anxiety about the stability of your work.

Unless you work in a particularly sensitive zone or niche, the tremors of change will be felt in other parts of your industry before your organization

A History Lesson

Review the history of the industry you are currently interested in. If you have colleagues with similar interests in the industry, ask them to do their own reviews. Share your findings. Address the following issues:

► **When and where did the industry first appear?**

► **What specific need or needs did the industry address at first?**

► **Who were some of the industry's earliest leaders?**

► **What professions did the leaders come from?**

► **What were the earliest organizations and jobs?**

► **What are the major categories of work in the industry? special markets? customers? niches?**

► **Who are the industry's leaders today? What organizations are they in?**

► **What new technologies and social trends will have the greatest future impact on this industry?**

► **Is the industry now growing, stable, or declining? How can you tell?**

or job is affected. If you're alert, you'll spot patterns in and around your industry that will eventually create pressure for new products, services, ways of packaging work, and so forth. If not, you'll be caught short and may even join the legions of unemployed workers.

Trends that have societal and economic implications usually appear in several places about the same time, as parts of larger, economy-wide movements and changes. Downsizing and reengineering, for example, grew out of a need for more efficiency in the global competitive environment. Certain "mini-trends" came from these larger movements:

▶ Smaller organizations

▶ Multiple employment modes: full-time, part-time, temporary, contract

▶ Interdisciplinary teams

▶ Alliances with companies providing secondary services

▶ Computerization

▶ Teleconferencing

▶ Telecommuting

Look for these trends if you are sizing up an industry. Industries that respond to them will be more vital than industries that hope things will go back to "business as usual." Many recent examples illustrate this point:

▶ Automobile mechanics who saw early that computers were the wave of the future in automobile design (fuel injection systems, engine control, antilock brakes, and sound systems) and went to school or learned on their own are now well positioned for leadership in automotive centers. Those still unfamiliar with computers will find it harder and harder to get high-paying jobs.

▶ Newspaper publishers who saw the growing use of electronic communications, the need for rapid dissemination of global news and up-to-date information, and the swell of workers reading computer screens rather than newspapers were the first to set up electronic newspapers. Those who waited to be sure electronic communication wasn't a fad are, no doubt, playing catch-up.

How well do your industry, your company, and your department keep up with trends that are obviously global and here to stay? A large industry has grown up around PCs, LANs, WANs, Web sites, color printers, and Internet marketing. Is your company still using mainframes or giving employees only grudging access to computers? If so, perhaps it's time to move on—or to become the professional, the master of computerization, who nudges, pushes, or leads the company successfully into the next century. You *don't* have to be an independent businessperson to be an entrepreneur.

Two Successful Trend Catchers

We must all become trend catchers, both in our own and in other industries. Whether or not you like a trend, if it gains momentum in and around your industry, you'd better pay attention. If you're smart, you'll learn to leverage the trend.

Paul and Terry Klaassen saw a need not directly related to their lifestyle. Frustrated by the nursing homes where Terry volunteered, they wondered about creating a more compassionate way to care for the elderly. Paul recalled visiting his elderly relatives in an assisted care house in his native Holland. In 1981 they founded Sunrise Assisted Living. The company builds appealing Victorian mansions instead of hospital-style, boxy institutions. With the number of Americans age 85 and older projected to increase from 3.7 million in 1996 to 6 million in 2010, the assisted-living concept is in its infancy. The Klaassens took Sunrise public in 1996, selling 40 percent of the company for $104 million. The stock price in 1997 is 153 times the expected 1997 earnings.

Seeing the Future—With Sense

There is no shortage today of self-styled prophets. Legions of futurists, corps of think tanks, and hordes of professional prognosticators bombard us with predictions through every media outlet. History teaches us to be wary about swallowing these assertions whole. For every Jules Verne hinting at the marvels of nuclear fusion a century in advance, there are several thousand Jeane Dixons predicting a global takeover by flying saucers. How can you extract a reliable estimate of what lies in store for your industry from this clamor of confident, yet often conflicting, predictions?

Industries are made up largely of people with similar interests. You can organize yourself and your colleagues to stay abreast of changes and problems in your industry and related industries by

▶ thinking, reading, and talking about the trends

▶ networking with others who share your interests

▶ joining industry and professional organizations

▶ attending conventions and seminars

Don't neglect independent research, either. Learn on your own by

▶ studying trade and industry magazines, books, CD-ROMs

▶ surfing the Internet

▶ reading annual reports of top companies in your industry

▶ seeking out annual industry ratings, analyses, and forecasts in periodicals such as *Fortune, Forbes,* the *Economist, Business Week,* and the *Wall Street Journal.*

You don't have to subscribe to these publications or slog through them cover to cover. Most good public or college libraries will have them on CD-ROM or microfilm. Search out the industry topics that interest you, using

NEW WORKER

- ▶ *Examine the relative importance of your profession or trade in researching any industry of interest.*
- ▶ *Check bookstores to see what new magazines and books are showing up in the industry. Scan industry journals.*
- ▶ *Be wary of taking a job where your profession is not core to the industry and organization.*
- ▶ *Identify the leaders in your profession. What industries hire them?*

IN TRANSITION

- ▶ *Before looking for organizations or jobs, do more research about which industries require your expertise.*
- ▶ *Pay particular attention to the core professions of the industry you are leaving or thinking of joining.*
- ▶ *Contact highly successful people in your profession who have made smart industry judgments.*
- ▶ *Be wary of staying in or returning to an industry where you've already been at risk.*

EXPERIENCED WORKER

- ▶ *If you are seasoned and masterly in a profession or trade, you can name your price and working conditions when you find the right industry.*
- ▶ *Check out industry associations for industry trends, hot topics, burning issues, and companies in need of your expertise.*
- ▶ *If you see yourself as seasoned but not a master, use your knowledge and experience in the industry to find masterly mentors and coaches.*
- ▶ *Set up a mastery track for yourself to jump-start your level of expertise.*

key words such as "retail trade," "alliances," and "global networks." You can print out selected articles on the spot or load them onto a diskette and take them home.

You can also access many of the above sources from your home if you have a computer with a modem. The major online information providers, CompuServe, America Online, and Prodigy, provide extensive access to a growing body of information sources, including the full text (with images) of most of the major news and business magazines, as well as to the Internet. Or you can access the Internet directly. By joining newsgroups on computers maintained by individuals, companies, nonprofit organizations, government agencies, libraries, and universities around the world, you can observe or participate in high-powered discussions among leading experts in many industries and professions.

These and other learning activities will help you improve and broaden your competencies, give you early indications of trends affecting the industry and your profession, and show you new niches where you might effectively market your services.

How Does Your Industry Stack Up?

A N INDUSTRY'S NEED FOR YOUR PROFESSION and its responsiveness to trends are, in general, the two most important factors that determine whether you can achieve a stable, rewarding career in the industry. Beyond these, there are many other factors to take into account. Keep in mind that you're not likely to find an industry in which all eight of the vitality indicators from page 143 are true; however, the better the fit, the more vital and powerful you'll find the industry.

Are Important Needs Served?

As you have seen, industries expand in response to various human needs. The more urgent those needs, and the closer your industry is to the point of customer contact or service, the more durable your industry will be.

Certain needs, health and the requirement for food, are basic to survival. Industries that fill these needs will never disappear. Indeed, with the growing affluence and improved technology created by many other industries, new niches open up every year in the food and health-care industries. We spend more on health foods, ethnic cuisine, specialty restaurants, gourmet ingredients, cooking schools, mental health, disease prevention, mind and body conditioning, and elder care than ever before. Some niches turn out to be fads; others, such as a more integrated, holistic, mind-body approach to medicine, appear to be more durable.

Focus on an industry of interest, either your current industry or one you are considering, and pinpoint the human needs this industry addresses. Given what you know of the social, political, economic, and technical issues affecting that need, how would you rank the importance of the industry now and in five years? This is the kind of broad perspective you need in order to anticipate the changes already affecting the industry.

Here are some questions to ask about the basic reasons for the industry's existence:

▶ What human needs does your industry serve?

▶ Would you rate these needs as highly survival related, moderately so, or relatively unimportant to survival?

▶ How have the expectations, products, and services around those needs changed in the last ten years? How do you expect them to change in the future? What new niches do you foresee to take care of those changes?

Changing Technologies, Changing Demands

When technology is rapidly changing in the playing field, an industry encounters both challenges to its survival and opportunities for prosperity. The same is true for a professional in the industry. Some competencies become marginal or obsolete; others grow more important or spring as if brand-new out of other competencies. A few decades ago, computer programming was a competency for a few scientists but otherwise an obscure hobby for dedicated enthusiasts. Now it is a multibillion-dollar profession that is growing and changing rapidly.

Even expert futurists are confounded by the rapidity of changing technology. Buck Rogers' ray gun has been achieved in the form of a laser; we got to the moon much more quickly than many experts believed possible. What can we learn from today's imaginative adventure tales, such as *Star Trek*? We may never surmount the energy, information, or moral challenges posed by the "transporter," but one invention that seems not out of the realm of possibility is the medical "tricorder," the hand-held instrument the doctor uses to diagnose illness and injury.

Far-fetched, you say? Look in at a modern hospital; you'll see a magnetic resonance imaging (MRI) instrument, a device that can explore the internal structure and functioning of the body without cutting it open or bombarding it with harmful X-rays. Computers went from dim-witted, house-sized monsters to swift, smart,

INDICATORS OF INDUSTRY VITALITY

1. **Serves an important need**

2. **Keeps up with changing technologies**

3. **Demonstrates high-growth potential**

4. **A variety of professional niches**

5. **Globally competitive**

6. **Locally competitive**

7. **Minimal regulations**

8. **Continues to expand the products and services**

hand-held PDAs (personal digital assistants) in fifty years; the same is happening in medical technology.

Of course, change is always met by resistance when it threatens to upset the political or societal status quo or the interests of large constituencies. Large organizations are often the least responsive to change. Once invested in a successful technology, any company finds it hard to anticipate the day when that technology will have to be discarded in favor of newer ones that work better and cost less. IBM and other leading computer makers lost their dominance when they failed to anticipate the demand for smaller, less-expensive personal computers. Bell Labs, inventors of cellular phone technology in the 1970s, failed to capture the initiative in the market, and Bell Labs' parent AT&T had to pay upstart McCaw Cellular several billion dollars twenty years later to buy it out.

Ask yourself these questions about your industry:

▶ What are some of the recent major technological shifts in the industry?

▶ What technologies will probably become obsolete in the industry in the next three to five years?

▶ What technologies in related industries might affect the industry?

▶ Which technologies will most affect my profession? My job?

▶ What new competencies do I need to learn in order to take advantage of these shifts in technology?

Measure Growth Potential— Peaked or Booming?

If you're looking for opportunity and excitement, look for today's version of the California Gold Rush—an industry that's just starting to take off, where the atmosphere is more like that of a Wild West boomtown than an Eastern metropolis. Look where things are changing—that's where the best opportunities, and the greatest risk, are found.

The phenomenon is also a lot like nature. In ecological terms, new niches are created where change is most rapid. An earthquake shakes loose a landslide (somebody starts mass-producing memory chips on silicon wafers), a new lake is created (microcomputer industry) in which hundreds of new species can live (Apple, HP, Intel, Compaq, Dell). The Gold Rush or earthquake industries today include telecommunications, entertainment, education, health care, computers, and building technologies. Keep in mind that you will encounter not only astonishing successes (VCRs, microwave ovens) but equally spectacular failures (been to any 3-D movies lately?). If you prefer predictability and stability, focus on industries that are growing slowly. If the industry is actually losing ground, it's time to look elsewhere.

These questions will guide you in exploring your industry's growth potential:

- ▶ What new niches are emerging?

- ▶ Which old niches are beginning to disappear?

- ▶ Would you recommend this industry to your children or your friends' children? Why or why not?

- ▶ What do leaders claim will be the most significant changes in the industry in the next decade?

Opportunity in Specialization

It's usually easier and less risky to move within an industry than between industries, especially if yours is a primary profession. Besides the leading companies, there are usually a variety of secondary markets, specialty suppliers, and so forth, that make your industry hospitable for long-term career vitality. The more diversified the industry, the more ways you can move without having to master a new profession.

On the other hand, rapid technological, regulatory, and economic changes often bring professionals new opportunities to switch industries. When the automobile industry was forced to meet new fuel economy and emissions standards in the '70s and '80s, the technical expertise it needed came from the aerospace industry. Aeronautical engineers designed low-drag shapes and minimized weight. Materials engineers made strong, lightweight parts from exotic materials such as carbon fibers and plastic. Aircraft controls systems engineers designed complex control devices to improve engine performance. Without this massive technology transfer from the aerospace industry, the American automotive industry might never have regained its prominent position in the world market, the national gasoline bill would have been much higher, and our environment would be a lot more damaged.

Think about the following points regarding work niches in your industry:

▶ What niches (small, large, specialized, global) is your industry known for?

▶ Do you work in a large, medium, or small niche?

▶ What other industry niches require your profession?

Global Competition

Competition is no longer just local or national—it's global. Instead of comparing your organization with others in the domestic industry, you must rate its practices and performance against an international standard. If your company is not prepared to stay on the leading edge of international industry practice, it is probably headed for a rude awakening, just as American autoworkers were rudely awakened by imports from Japan in the 1970s. Failure to see the emergence of efficient foreign producers practically destroyed the steel industry. It's just now recovering, and it may never regain its former vitality. Your career plans will be better served in those sectors of the industry that are actively seeking world-class performance.

Global competition is a healthy influence on domestic industries. The breakup of AT&T's telecommunications monopoly in 1984 stimulated enormous growth and job development. An industry that had seen only sluggish technological advancement and market expansion exploded into a multitude of companies offering new goods and services and new price and cost structures.

Use these questions to examine the competitive position of your industry in the worldwide economy:

► What companies excel in your industry? Are they domestic or foreign?

► Does your organization excel in global competition?

► How has global industry leadership changed in the past ten years?

► Which companies are talked about as the future leaders in the industry?

Local Competition

Global competition is the driving force in today's job markets. But for most of us, our immediate concern is who we are up against locally. After all, if you're raising a family and building a career in Dallas or Detroit, you're probably not interested in moving to Japan or Germany. You'd just as soon have your industry thrive in your own country. Can your industry continue to satisfy the human needs it was created to meet in the face of technological competition from other domestic industries? Can your company outrun its nearest domestic competitors and help the national industry remain competitive in the world arena? Look for work in an industry that is staying abreast of world trends, and in an organization that is in a leadership position in the local market. Industries that are closely coupled with mainstream business activity—those with a major economic impact—naturally have more resources to deploy and offer more variety (market niches) and more diverse career opportunities. Industries with a small or declining role in the economy offer fewer career options.

Answer these questions about your industry's local competitiveness:

▶ How is the industry characterized in terms of the economic health of the country?

▶ What other domestic industries are encroaching on the human needs and customer base this industry serves?

▶ What expansion of workers and work is occurring in the local industry? Which niches are on the increase?

▶ What shrinkage or outsourcing of work is occurring in the local industry? Which niches are in the greatest decline domestically?

Regulatory Impact

Government regulation and influence pervade business at all levels these days—from overt and direct, as in taxation, to subtle and difficult to quantify, in the form of subsidies, insurance, and regulatory compliance reporting. Wherever an industry affects or is affected by major societal issues such as health care, environmental safeguards, and allocation of public resources, governments will be involved. This is one of the important functions of government: protecting the public interest against harm from private interests.

As you look toward the future of your career, consider that local and national governments worldwide will be both regulators and customers of some industries. You may be doing work that is either hindered or created by the needs of governments. Such work is often slow and difficult to change, even when the need for improvements in products and procedures is blatantly evident. Because the federal government's purchasing procedures take so long, for example, the functioning and efficiency of many U.S. government agencies is severely hobbled by computers that are always several generations out of date.

Governments all over the world are struggling to balance regulation for the common good against the obvious benefits of free, fair, robust competition. However such issues are decided, the dominant trend is toward open competition, unconstrained by government partnership. When you choose an industry to commit professional expertise, remember that the smaller the organization and the farther from government regulation, the faster it can adapt and respond to competitive pressures.

Here are some considerations regarding government regulation of your industry:

▶ To what extent do federal or local regulations control the industry?

▶ Have regulations been decreasing or increasing in the industry? How does this trend affect creativity and productivity?

▶ What implications do you see for the increased or decreased cost of doing business?

▶ What direct implications are there for you in your own work?

Expanding Products and Services

The number of new products and services generated is a good measure of an industry's growth and health. When an industry expands and new niches pop up all over the map, you can be sure there's research and development and entrepreneurial activity—in short, opportunity.

Not long ago, most office equipment was designed to be used in the offices of large organizations. More and more of today's offices, however, are found in basements, kitchens, and converted double garages, with mobile outposts in cars, planes, and trains. The sizes, shapes, colors, costs, portability, and mobility of offices has never been so diverse.

As organizations outsource more of their administrative functions, the office services industry is expanding. Quick-print businesses have sprung up on every corner. Kinko's slogan, "The new way to office," means graphic support, word processing, printing, and delivery—services that secretaries used to provide. Printers don't just apply ink to paper, they also offer consultative graphic design, storage, assembly—even drop-ship orders, a result of just-in-time inventory control systems. As work and information handling shifts to the Internet, the industry will change again—and yet again if the "paperless office" ever becomes a reality.

Here are some questions about your industry's expansion capabilities:

▶ How many products and services generated by your industry can you name that weren't available a couple of years ago?

▶ What new products and services are being invented by your industry now?

▶ Where do most of the innovations in the industry come from?

▶ What are the implications for your profession of business expansion or contraction in your industry?

▶ What new products or services could you champion in your own organization or profession?

Watching the industry ring of the Web of Work will help you spot the early signs of impending change before the ramifications are felt in your own

NEW WORKER

▶ *Use the eight indicators as a guide for interview questions and to conduct other research about the industry.*

▶ *Read trade magazines to follow rankings of various industries.*

▶ *Use whatever sources you can find to build your understanding of and perspective on any industry that interests you.*

IN TRANSITION

▶ *These indicators may shed some light on the questions you are facing and give you insight into the whole system.*

▶ *If you have recently experienced or are anticipating downsizing or right-sizing, the indicators will serve as objective measures for deciding whether to stay in the industry.*

▶ *You can also use the indicators to assess growing industries that need your professional expertise.*

EXPERIENCED WORKER

▶ *If you are already working in a given industry, use the indicators to assess the future vitality of that industry.*

▶ *If the industry is growing slowly or declining, you might want to explore other industries that could use your professional expertise or trade.*

organization or job. For even more warning, build a support network of fellow Web watchers in your industry. If you are in a core profession and aware of what's happening in your industry, you're well positioned to maximize your mastery and marketability, even to become a leader, by switching industries or organizations.

PART V

Organizations

*"Work is that which puts us in touch with others,
not so much at the level of personal interaction,
but at the level of service in the community."*

—*Matthew Fox*

Your overview of the Web of Work can teach you to plan your work life in terms of professions and industries, the most stable and enduring parts of the whole. But once you know generally where you are going, you have to be practical. Look for organizations that will value your contribution and pay you for your work. As members of a civilized society, we plan and conduct our daily lives in, around, and with the help of organizations. They are an essential feature, perhaps even part of the definition, of civilization. So there will always be organizations that can use your competencies.

In every industry, however, organizations come and go. Some rise and fall in a matter of weeks or months; others endure for generations. Any organization that intends to survive must adapt to changing economic, technological, and societal conditions. To do so, it must continually reshape its work; it creates and eliminates jobs. During the course of your work life, you will probably associate with several organizations. The days of the employer for life are behind us. So the question arises: How do you find an organization that is likely to be around, and keep you around, long enough to help you achieve career success before *you decide* to move on?

These days, many things about organizations are changing, but there are several constants that have to do with organizational permanence and suitability for your career. This section presents eight indicators that will help *you assess the vitality of organizations. It will show you how to answer the following basic questions:*

► *What is the character of the organization—form, shape, feel, size, and so forth?*

► *What basic need does the organization serve?*

► *Does it fit your passion, purpose, values, and profession?*

► *What kind of partner will it be?*

NEW WORKER

► *When you visit a potential employer, investigate the organization's culture, values, and mission by asking questions and observing.*

► *Think of your potential employer as a possible partner. Does the chemistry work? Do you "fit"?*

► *If you're already working in an organization, use the information in this section to assess the fit. Is it good now? How might it be in the future?*

IN TRANSITION

► *If you have left an organization recently for any reason, what other justifications for leaving can you find in these chapters?*

► *If you're thinking of leaving an organization, use this section to help in making your decision.*

► *If you've been asked to leave an organization, use the information in these chapters to help you understand why.*

► *Develop your own checklist of things you require in future organizations.*

EXPERIENCED WORKER

► *How well does your current organization stack up to your changing needs and requirements? Is it a viable partner for the future?*

► *What other organizations fit some of the criteria in these chapters?*

► *How might you use your reputation and support network to investigate other organizations?*

► *Could you package your talent in a way that brings you work opportunities in a wider variety of organizations?*

In Pursuit of the Right Organization

YOU LIKELY WILL WORK FOR MORE than one organization in your lifetime. As you grow older, you will probably find that an organization that suited you when you were learning your skills and competencies no longer fits your needs as a married person with a growing family, as a mature professional, or as a master in your field. You may even find it possible, perhaps even necessary, to start your own organization to achieve career satisfaction.

Your choice of organizations rests primarily on your profession, of course, and the industries that need your professional abilities to meet a particular set of human needs. Within an industry, some organizations will be declining as they fail to adapt and compete; others will be expanding, innovating, opening new niches for you to fill. Your ability to meet the changing needs of your industry will affect your chances of finding work that gives you professional satisfaction.

Finding personal satisfaction in your work, though, takes more than a good professional fit. Your organization must be compatible with your personal values, core interests, family commitments, and financial needs. If you love your work but are finding it increasingly difficult to spend time with your family, if you are professionally accomplished but don't like the social or environmental consequences of what your company does, you will find it difficult to be happy in your work.

Is Your Organization a Good Fit for You?

This chapter will help you match what counts for you with what counts for an organization. There are three basic questions you need to answer to see if your current or potential organization fits your needs:

▶ Does your personal purpose align with your organization's purpose?

▶ Are your values in sync with those of your organization?

▶ Are your professional and core competencies essential to your organization?

If you can answer yes to all three of these questions, you are more likely to be creative, productive, and at peace in the organization. Misalignment in these areas manifests itself in many ways: restlessness, low productivity, emotional turmoil, depression, ill health, cynicism, addiction, even violence.

You and I know people, perhaps friends or relatives, who suffer a slow death of the spirit and sink into physical decline working in an organization that doesn't fit their values, interests, and strengths.

Align Your Purpose with the Organization's

Money is not the only reward for work. Most people want their work to matter to the world—to feel that what they do contributes in unique ways to the life, health, satisfaction, or well-being of others. Throughout our lives we strive to leave our mark in arenas we care about. Some people are fortunate to know what they want to do from an early age. Others of us go through several companies and jobs, learning by trial and error what we like and don't like to do, before we find our calling.

My stepdaughter, Marilyn, a graduate of Columbia Law School, had a high-paying position in a prestigious law firm representing wealthy clients, but her dream was to help people of lesser means. She offered her services to an organization that suited her mission but was told they had no positions available. Nevertheless, she set herself a deadline for telling her firm she was leaving. One week before that deadline arrived, she got a call from her ideal organization: they were hiring. Was she still interested? She works there today, happy and fulfilled, helping people improve the quality of their lives. Organizations that fit your personal purpose in life sometimes fall into your lap, but more often, like Marilyn, you have to search for them. Other people find they have to create their own—and that is the genesis of many new organizations.

An organization's purpose is its reason for being. Read the mission or vision statement. This will tell you at least what goal—which human need— the organization originally harnessed and focused its human energy to meet. Try to determine whether the organization still strives toward that purpose, still guides and inspires its workers to accomplish a greater good. Then decide whether that mission matches yours.

Choose an organization you care about. Find answers to the following questions:

▶ What is the organization's mission or purpose?

▶ What human needs does the organization address? How does it address them?

▶ What would its workers say is the purpose of the organization?

▶ How do its customers talk about the services they receive?

▶ How do competitors and the trade journals speak about the organization?

Don't just go by what the organization *says;* look carefully at what it does. Trust your instincts. If you're new, ask people with more experience in the company. If you're in transition, choose a specific organization to study—your last organization, the one you are thinking of leaving, or one you are considering joining. If you are an experienced worker, look at your organization or at one you might want to move to.

Now, review the personal purpose statement that you wrote in chapter 4. Consider the following questions:

▶ What basic human needs are you predisposed to serve?

▶ What legacy do you want to leave?

▶ What do you want people to say about your contribution to them?

Finally, compare your purpose statement with what you know about the organization or organizations in question:

► In what ways is your purpose aligned with the organization's purpose?

► How is it out of sync with the organization's purpose?

► How does this misalignment express itself at work? at home? personally?

► Are there other organization(s) where you see a greater alignment of purpose with your own? What would it take to work there? What results would you foresee?

I have worked with hundreds of people who have given up on their passion and purpose, who have sold out because they didn't think they could find or create the right organization. And I've worked with hundreds of others who, like Marilyn, have put their careers on the line to find or create an organization whose purpose they can work with in harmony. The latter are much happier and contribute more to their community.

Compare Your Values with the Organization's

Values are the deeply held beliefs that guide our day-to-day actions and our long-term decisions. They motivate us, and they guide the moral choices we make in achieving our purpose. This is true of both individuals and organizations. Personal values are often part of an individual's cultural or spiritual heritage and are instilled through education. An organization's values typically reflect the ethics and culture of its founders and are sometimes expressed in a vision statement or credo. Recognizing and naming your core values is an important step in living life harmoniously. If you live in harmony with your values, you experience peace, calm, and clarity. If you ignore or violate them, you may suffer anxiety, burnout, or worse.

Every organization has a culture—values, written or unwritten, that embody its relationship with its employees, its competitors, and its community, and that guide how its workers conduct business. Companies with very strong cultures go to great lengths, either in the selection process or through indoctrination, to ensure that new workers will fit into its culture.

Organization Values

Autonomy and entrepreneurship	**Pioneer new solutions**
Being out front	**Price leads the way**
Continual self-improvement	**Take risks**
Corporate social responsibility	**The customer is always right**
Family comes first	**We have an open-door policy**
Heroic customer service	**We value and seek differences**
No suggestion is too small	**We're a family**
Partnerships are our hallmark	**Win, no matter what**

The statements or slogans in the box imply certain organization values. Each sets up expectations about practices, processes, and the values of its workers. Read them; circle the ones that sound like values of your current organization or an organization you are interested in joining. It may help to interview people working there; ask them specifically about the organization's values.

Now reflect on which of your personal values are aligned with the organization's values. Look at the slogans you circled.

▶ Which of your values fit the organization's values?

▶ Which of your values don't fit or are missing?

▶ How many of your top ten values are in sync with the organization's values?

Alignment of vision and values becomes more important as we mature. We all want to be true to ourselves, but the more we accept our mortality, the more we are driven to accomplish something of importance and to achieve inner satisfaction.

Your Profession and the Organization's Mission

To become lean, mean, and competitive, companies are learning to direct more of their energy and resources toward a few primary products or services and less toward secondary functions. By focusing on what they do best and avoiding niches where they have no deep expertise or mature talent, they can improve efficiency and quality, and respond more quickly to changes in technology or the marketplace.

Being a high-performing organization requires hiring, educating, and retaining people in a few professions that are directly connected to achieving the organization's mission. Functions and processes that are not crucial in one company—pension-plan administration, advertising, logistics management, to name a few—are outsourced to companies with these functions as their missions.

An outstanding example of this trend is the success of Kinko's. This office support chain provides printing, copying, word processing, desktop publishing, publication design, graphic arts, and project management. Larger organizations used to provide these internally, generally with lower quality and efficiency than Kinko's—a business with "office support" as its primary mission.

In addition to opening up opportunities for new organizations and jobs to provide these support functions, outsourcing trends gives more professionals the opportunity to work in organizations that are among the best at what they do. Instead of being a support professional in an unwieldy conglomerate, a worker can be a core professional in any of a number of smaller, leaner support companies.

A company that wishes to focus on its mission and strategies can now ally itself with another company that provides necessary support services; both companies thereby achieve maximum speed and flexibility as employees work in their core professions. This gives you, at least potentially, more organizations and more jobs in which your competencies are a primary requirement.

When you assess an organization's need for your competencies, reflect on the following issues:

▶ What are the core professions needed in the organization?

▶ What are the secondary professions for the organization?

▶ What organization strategies, products, or services require your expertise?

▶ If you left, would your expertise have to be replaced?

▶ Name five other organizations that need your talent and expertise.

If you are just beginning your career or thinking of changing organizations, these are the key factors to investigate. Once you've decided that the organization is a good fit, you can use the eight organization viability indicators given in chapter 12 to assess the quality and viability of the organization.

Is Your Organization Viable?

Sense of Purpose

Leaders in Core Professions

Supports Research and Development

Exhibits Growth Potential

Promotes Learning Culture

Shares Wealth with Employees

Values Open Communication

Shares Authority

*L*ET'S SUPPOSE YOU FIND A PLACE in an organization that fits you well, where you're comfortable and can take satisfaction in your work. You work there six months. Suddenly, there's a company-wide announcement: due to slow growth and declining profits, your company is being dismantled by the parent organization.

How can you know in advance whether your company has what it takes to make it over the long haul? You can use the eight indicators of organization vitality discussed in this chapter, which are based on the performance and experience of many of the fastest-growing, most-admired, and most-successful companies in the world. If an organization needs your competencies and fits your values and purpose, take some time to assess its future. After reading through the discussion on each of the viability indicators, assess the health of your current organization or the one you are thinking of joining or leaving. This will help you plan your long-term career strategy.

Sense of Purpose

Perhaps at some time in your life you've experienced the joy of participating in and contributing to a cause—have even gone without food or sleep—because of the galvanizing force of a leader's vision. With your purpose and values bound to those of your organization, you may have been inspired to heroic levels of creativity, productivity, and service. This sense of common cause in an organization is what separates the great from the merely good. With nothing to energize and inspire them, people can become petty, self-serving, silo-minded, bored, lazy, or simply demoralized. Organizations eventually fail when their workers lack a shared purpose.

Most organizations and their workers share a mission at start-up and in their early years. Once they have grown and matured, it can be harder to maintain a mission focus. Leaders and managers must constantly question,

**INDICATORS OF
ORGANIZATION VITALITY**

1. **Sense of purpose**

2. **Leaders come from core
   professions**

3. **Conducts research and
   development**

4. **Demonstrates growth potential**

5. **Learning culture**

6. **Wealth sharing**

7. **Information sharing**

8. **Power sharing**

discuss, and reinforce that sense of purpose in their teams. Good leaders accomplish this by giving people meaningful work that directly relates to that purpose and by helping them see the results of their labors.

Good leaders also demonstrate that they share the concerns of every worker. What counts in an organization, what matters to its leaders, may be subtle, but it is easily sensed by its people after a short time. At Southwest Airlines, a company known for its esprit de corps, pilots and executives pitch in and handle baggage in a crunch; employees at all levels routinely give their own time to help stranded or disabled passengers. All feel a sense of ownership in their organization and are fiercely loyal to the company and to one another. Effective leaders let people know what behavior is valued. When workers can take pride in the purpose and values of their organization, their commitment to achieving results goes up. They eagerly "go the extra mile" for customers.

Answer these questions regarding your organization's mission:

▶ Can you state the purpose of the organization in a sentence?

▶ Are you, or would you be, proud to be aligned with this organization's purpose and values?

▶ Ask five co-workers what they consider the purpose of the organization.

Leaders in Core Professions

What do Edwin Land, Estée Lauder, and Eli Lilly have in common (besides the monograms on their bath towels)? Each was an expert in his or her profession who founded a successful company. Edwin Land invented the Polaroid Land Camera; Estée Lauder used a family formula to found a successful line of cosmetics; Eli Lilly, a physician during the Civil War, devised new ways of encapsulating doses of medicines.

It doesn't take a master to create a successful company, but it helps. A recent study of over seventeen hundred fast-growing start-up companies revealed that most of their CEOs had more than ten years' experience in their industry.[1] A sense of history is part of what gives great leaders that seemingly intuitive sense of what will and won't work. They can "smell" opportunity and timing.

Experience in running a company helps, too. The same study showed that many of the most successful new companies were headed by entrepreneurs who had started other businesses. Effective managers and technical leaders are synthesizers who can bring resources together, who are aware of the risks of running a company, and who can recognize when people are trying to solve today's problems with yesterday's solutions. Their professional background gives them a historical perspective on customers' needs and an ability to distinguish between fads and significant trends. Their companies are usually at the forefront of their industries.

Belonging to an organization that is seen as best in class by competitors, customers, and workers gives you a strong foundation for developing depth and breadth in your career. When you look for such a company, let the following questions guide your research:

▶ Can you name some industry-leading professionals in the organization?

▶ Who are the idea pioneers in the organization?

▶ Who are the best in the company? Are they some of the best world-wide?

▶ How is talent development rewarded?

Supports Research and Development

Leaders must balance the short-term and the long-term needs of current and future customers. Yielding too easily to the pressures to make fast profits can jeopardize the future of a company. Those that want to be around in the future commit time, money, and resources to R&D.

Systems and practices to encourage and reward entrepreneurial spirit should be built into the organization. One of the major reasons talented employees leave organizations is that their ideas for future products, services, or innovations are not given a serious hearing. 3M, known for its innovative products, believes that innovation and entrepreneurship come in various shapes and sizes and structures its research accordingly. Beyond its investment in traditional research projects, it allows its researchers to spend 15 percent of their time working on any idea that interests them, funds other projects that are expected to produce profitable products within a year or two, and gives its researchers the freedom to gather whatever resources they need.[2]

At Xerox, communication is a key cultural value. Engineers, researchers, and managers working on related projects share office space and information sources. Marketing people are assigned to research projects, technology experts are placed in other divisions, researchers communicate freely with key customers—all to ensure that the technology meets consumer needs.[3]

Look for an organization that publicizes its business plans and forecasts. Knowing the company's research plans helps keep you in touch with industry trends, new technologies, growth opportunities, and changes in the demand for crucial competencies and skills. You can spot the need for your services in other parts of the organization and prepare to compete for coveted assignments. Making such information accessible is one indicator of a company that is committed to maximizing the talents and helping the career development of its employees.

When you assess an organization's commitment to research and development, ask the following questions:

▶ What percentage of the organization's income is put into R&D?

▶ In what ways does the organization support communication between researchers, product developers, marketing, and customers?

▶ How does the organization encourage and reward entrepreneurship?

▶ How does the organization stay abreast of social trends, technical trends, demographic trends, financial trends, regulatory trends, and customer trends?

Exhibits Growth Potential

The growth potential of an organization used to be judged on the basis of its size, number of employees, market share, R&D investment, location, and competitive edge. Today, most analysts recognize that bigger is not necessarily better. The financial health of a company involves many factors not directly related to size—as General Motors, IBM, and Sears can tell you from recent experience.

But even the traditional measures of an organization's financial health, such as a high operating profit ratio, a low debt-to-equity ratio, rising gross profit margins, or cash on hand, are not proof that a company will survive in the long term. Given the volatility of the market, the ferocity of the competition, the rapid pace of technological change, and the number of powerful entrepreneurial ventures that have been launched on a shoestring, today's success story can quickly become tomorrow's sob story. For career security, look for an organization that fosters an entrepreneurial mindset. The most reliable organizations concentrate on products and services that will be needed by a large number of customers well into the future.

Here are some questions to ask yourself about an organization's growth potential:

► How well does the organization stack up on the traditional financial measures?

► Does the organization express clearly what it does best, and the core processes for fulfilling its mission?

► What trends does the organization expect to be affected by? How does it plan to deal with them?

► Where does the organization compete best, locally or globally?

Promotes Learning Culture

Large organizations have traditionally invested some of their resources in the training and development of their workers, with the focus on individual skill building. Until recently, only research organizations paid much attention to organizational learning. Today, however, to cope with the speed of change and to pass along crucial organizational wisdom to a highly mobile work-force, companies find they have to invest in both kinds of learning. Processes change quickly in developing industries where jobs are being created; products and services grow obsolete faster wherever a developing technology finds a new application. A worker must learn continuously to stay competitive—and by the same token, an organization must foster that learning in order to compete successfully.

Organizations that understand the value of continual employee learning find many ways of teaching their workers or supporting their efforts to learn on their own. Self-directed learning, development assignments and projects, benchmarking best practices, shadowing "the best," and reimbursing employees for job-related course fees are popular methods. For many companies, learning new competencies and developing new approaches or new products are also tied to reward systems.

► The Canadian Imperial Bank of Commerce has developed competency models for customer service employees—then abolished all training. Armed with their lists of competencies, employees are responsible for learning what they don't yet know or enhancing what they do know to perform their current jobs. They can use books and software at their branch learning room, and managers are instructed to let them shadow colleagues to learn from them.[4]

► Polaroid pipes job-related courses into its offices from nearby Harvard, MIT, and Northeastern University and has hooked up a satellite relay from the National Technological University, a consortium of thirty-nine institutions that offers advanced degrees in disciplines such as materials science. As an added incentive, Polaroid pegs raises and promotions to acquiring new skills.[5]

Employee education is routinely encouraged and facilitated in most large companies, but the importance of being a learning organization has only recently become widely recognized, especially since the publication of Peter Senge's *The Fifth Discipline* in 1990. Learning organizations learn from the knowledge and experience of their workers. They become adept at translating new knowledge into new behaviors, policies, and procedures. This can be done in a variety of ways, but the most promising new practices come from the widespread computerization of industry. The ability to store and manipulate large volumes of information allows organizations to design expert systems that will store, build, and pass on organizational learning.

► At Xerox, when a technician finds a part that failed, he or she logs the fact into an information base that will guide engineers to problem areas when they design a new copier.[6]

► To alert engineers more quickly to design defect and regulatory issues, Hughes Space & Communications has begun a pilot project that will use groupware to connect existing databases of lessons learned.[7]

▶ Root Learning is developing poster-sized "learning maps" depicting core processes to guide question formats for study groups learning the basics of the business.

For long-term career stability and advancement, look for an organization that values learning, both by its people and by its systems and practices. Learning is the only way a professional and an organization can stay abreast of the changes that occur in the rapidly evolving Web of Work. When investigating the attitude your current or prospective organization has toward learning, try to find answers to these questions:

▶ How is individual learning recognized and rewarded?

▶ What are the tuition aid policies and practices?

▶ What practices are in place to encourage organizational learning?

▶ What structures and systems are in place to pass on wisdom and know-how, so that people in other parts of the organization profit from learning everywhere?

Shares Wealth with Employees

Among the top companies in America you will find a growing recognition that the best work and service requires a true partnership. The most progressive companies address family issues such as child care, work hours, and job sharing with an eye toward keeping good employees and making them more productive. They know there is a high correlation between company profitability and employee partnership. Organizations that haven't yet learned this lesson are losing their best people to organizations that have.

A recent Coopers & Lybrand survey of fast-growing companies found that 80 percent had employee-participation programs. Of these companies, the 66 percent that considered their programs "essential" or "very important" ranked consistently higher on plans for growth than did the 34 percent who rated their programs "somewhat important" or "unimportant."[8]

The organization's concern for its employees, their families, and the community manifests itself in many different ways.

▶ Profit-sharing and gain-sharing programs have increased dramatically, as have employee stock ownership plans (ESOP). Physicians Sales and Service, with 1995 sales over $200 million, has an ESOP, operates incentive stock-option and nonqualified stock-option plans, and recently started a share purchase plan outside the ESOP. Employees also participate in decision making.[9]

▶ At Semco, a leading Brazilian manufacturing company, 23 percent of profits are distributed to employees. Six people, including a woman, rotate as CEO in six-month terms.[10]

▶ Many organizations now have day-care facilities on premises. Others make it easy for parents to drop off and pick up their children.

▶ On-site fitness centers and subsidized health club memberships are other means by which organizations are providing for the overall health and well-being of their employees.

You want not only a fulfilling career but a chance for you and your family to share in the benefits the company derives from your work. Look for companies that consider the well-being of their workers, their communities, and the world among their major responsibilities. Look for companies that share the wealth and care for the environment, and whose workers respond by being loyal, innovative, and inspired.

Ask the following questions about any organization you are interested in:

► How does the organization share profits? with whom?

► What benefits does the organization give? health care? child care? parent care? tuition aid?

► Does the organization institute policies and practices to protect the environment?

Values Open Communication

The ease with which communication happens, both internally and with customers, tells you much about whether an organization is open, adaptable, and responsive to market trends and employee input. Easy information access is a principal factor behind the new organization's flatter power structure: fewer layers of managers are needed to obtain, process, analyze, and distribute information internally. Productivity is closely linked with how readily employees can update their technical skills, communicate problems and solutions to one another, and respond to customer requests. When information is fully shared, the company's partnership with its employees is reflected in its partnership with customers.

The personal computer is now the communication tool of choice. More than a supplement to the telephone system, a computer can connect each worker fully with all the information the organization has on hand, plus the universe of information beyond. Local- and wide-area networks let you communicate without moving out of your office. E-mail is faster than the postal service, more convenient and more versatile than the telephone. When its full potential is realized—that is, when its software is not in need of troubleshooting or upgrading and its operator fully trained—the computer is a productivity generator.

In virtually every organization, the investment in tools that improve information flow (reliable phone systems, computer networks, e-mail, Internet connectivity) is a key indicator of commitment to productivity. The less energy employees need to expend to get the information they need to do their job properly, the more energy they will have to come up with innovative product and service ideas that further the organization's purpose.

If the following statements are true, consider the organization a powerful, productive user of communication tools:

▶ Communicating crucial information to other employees throughout the organization is easy.

▶ Answers to work questions are quickly available.

▶ Information flows laterally among team members and colleagues.

▶ Communicating with customers is fast and easy.

▶ Technology is used to increase productivity.

▶ Technology is used to connect with partners and allies.

▶ Employees are encouraged to continuously update technical skills.

In its most advanced form, the new connectivity extends outside the company, both upstream and downstream. As the interdependence between suppliers, manufacturers, service providers, and customers grows, the boundaries between them blur. Many organizations go to extraordinary lengths to build and maintain long-term business partnerships. Fewer manufacturers actually make what they sell. Instead, they build strong alliances with contract manufacturers, who become crucial collaborators. For example, 70 percent of a Dodge Intrepid arrives at the assembly line as finished modules from outside suppliers.[11]

More and more, the communication between these business partners occurs online, through computers, just as it does inside the organizations. The easier this communication, the better; it reduces errors and misunderstandings, increases support, and benefits productivity all around.

Here are some questions to consider when judging how well an organization shares information:

▶ How many workers have PCs or terminals?

▶ How easy is access to computers, faxes, databases, and online networks?

▶ Is the communication and database technology compatible across the organization?

▶ Are you linked with customers and suppliers through e-mail?

Shares Authority

When the flow of information within the organization is truly free, not only does it keep employees informed about what's going on, it also transmits feedback to managers. The most enlightened organizations exploit this information to the fullest. They know that employees who feel their opinions and expertise are taken seriously and acted upon are employees who are more likely to be passionate and professional in their work.

In the best companies in the world, employees are genuinely involved in making decisions that affect their jobs. The most committed workers—the ones every company values most—derive satisfaction from having a say in whatever affects them and their careers. When their expertise and experience tell them there's a better way to do a job, they expect the people in charge to listen to them. They are also willing to risk a certain amount of career uncertainty to gain a degree of control over their own lives.[12]

In your organization or in any organization you are thinking of joining, how much power does the employee have? These questions will help you assess this factor:

► What kind of access does the worker have to organization leaders and decision makers?

► How does the organization foster employee participation?

► What structures and systems are in place for hearing and acting on employee ideas and recommendations?

► Do people feel they can innovate, challenge the status quo, push, and take risks?

These eight vitality indicators will help you assess the strength, adaptability, and durability of an organization. Keep in mind, however, that longevity does not necessarily mean an organization will stay the way you like it, or even remain in the same geographic area. Just as your needs change as you mature, your organization's requirements may change as it adapts to changing technologies, competition, and other economic factors. The human needs you both serve will, of course, always be there, even if you and the organization change the way you deal with them.

PART VI

Jobs

> *"Choose a job you love and you'll never work a day in your life."*
>
> —*Confucius*

A job is the least stable, least enduring, most fragile part of the Web of Work. It's like a single grain of sand on the beach. The wind blows, the surf crashes, the dunes shift. In a year, a grain of sand gets ground down, swirled around, moved yards or miles down the beach, perhaps washed out to sea and lost. Yet, like an industry, the beach remains; and like an organization, the dune manages to last several years, even as it moves slowly down the shoreline.

What, exactly, is a job? Generally, it's a cluster of related tasks or responsibilities brought together in a convenient person-sized package to take care of a specific, short-term need. Examples are clerking in a convenience store, operating a TV camera or a printing press, and receiving visitors and answering phones in an office. Jobs are such a part of our vocabulary and our experience of work that, in fact, we have come to equate jobs with work.

And that's the rub—if you look only at the short-term organizational need, you're ignoring the long-term, basic human need that brought into existence your organization, your industry, and especially your profession, your kind of work. That's why you should think in broader terms than a job—you should keep your eye on the rest of the Web of Work all the time. Otherwise, as soon as any of the tasks, responsibilities, or customers change, your job might just shift out from under you or disappear.

In the next three chapters we will explore the significance of the job. But

NEW WORKER

▶ Evaluate all jobs in terms of the human needs you want to address and the professions in which they reside.

▶ Don't let money become the only driver in your decisions.

IN TRANSITION

▶ Take a good look at jobs you've held. Did they foster growth and mastery in your profession, or were they a series of repetitive tasks affording little new learning?

▶ How well have you weathered changes in technology and job reengineering?

▶ Study the eight indicators of job vitality in chapter 15. Use them to assess future jobs and to create your own jobs that meet the criteria.

EXPERIENCED WORKER

▶ You are probably in a position to create your own future work or to redesign your current work to meet your needs. Use the eight indicators of vital jobs to assess your work today and create new work for the future.

▶ You can also coach young workers in structuring their jobs to acquire professional depth and breadth.

our focus will not be "How to Find a Job" or "How to Get a Better Job"— plenty of other books have been written about those topics. Instead, we will explore the idea of finding work that is suitable, satisfying, and stable among all the threads of the Web of Work.

Jobs can either be gateways to personal satisfaction or tunnels to boredom. Just because certain jobs are on the increase doesn't mean they are channels for professional mastery. You will see the importance of studying the learning possibilities before signing up.

A discussion of the pros and cons of reengineering and technology will shed some light on your current work situation. You'll also see how break-throughs in other industries affect jobs throughout the Web of Work.

The eight indicators of job vitality outlined in chapter 15 will help you evaluate past job experience and show you what you should find out before taking any job. The indicators can also show you ways to reengineer your current job or create a new job to address an unmet need.

The Fragility of Jobs

*T*HE "JOB" AS WE KNOW IT took hold during the Industrial Revolution. Breaking down work into a sequence of low-skilled tasks, or jobs, made a jobholder just another cog in the factory-floor machinery. The effect was felt not only in manufacturing but in all industries. Efficient use of assembly lines demanded that all work be divided into discrete tasks, with each worker doing as few of these tasks as possible. One worker—an unskilled or semiskilled specialist, as it were—would do one thing, over and over, as many times as he or she could be made to do it.

The problem from the beginning was that being part of an assembly line left little room for creativity, quality, or job satisfaction. Quality suffered because workers had little or no investment in their work; many never even knew what the final product was. Job satisfaction suffered for the same reason. Aside from drawing a paycheck, what satisfaction can you derive from a mind-numbing job in which you never see the fruits of your labors? What basic human need are you serving by stamping envelopes in a mail room, turning an unending series of pulleys on a lathe, or crunching long columns of numbers eight hours a day, year after year?

Another consequence of this fragmentation of work is more apparent than ever because of the accelerating rate of change in all industries. When parts of an assembly line become obsolete, they are quickly replaced by more efficient components. This includes jobholders. Telephone switchboard operators, shorthand stenographers, railroad firemen, middle managers everywhere—all have become or are becoming obsolete parts of old-style assembly lines. Not too long ago you could make a career out of a single job. Now jobs tend to come and go in a few years, months, or weeks.

Back to the Future

The one great technological change that is beginning to transform all work is, strangely enough, rolling back this most dehumanizing aspect of the Industrial Revolution. Computers, even in their infancy, are already proving faster, cheaper, and more reliable in accomplishing routine, repetitive tasks. People are being rediscovered in all their complexity and intelligence.

Humans, it seems, are better than computers at seeing similarities between things that aren't the same—and at being intuitive. A computer can solder resistor A to terminal B better, faster, and for longer hours than a person can—but it takes a person to teach the computer how, to figure out ways to speed up the process, and to intuit that you could make the product better by replacing resistor A with resistor C. A human can instantly recognize the face of a steady customer, connect it with a name and a history, read subtle shadings of mood and meaning on it, and respond in an almost infinite variety of ways to its owner's request. These skills are as yet beyond the capability of even the most powerful computer. A human who can do all this is a skilled professional—just as in the glory days of craftsmen, before the Industrial Revolution.

This is the way work is evolving—in a way, back to the future. And this is the way you must learn to see work, not as a scattering of unrelated tasks or jobs but as a spectrum of related skills that you must master to take advantage of your uniquely human strengths—insight, intuition, and the ability to learn.

The Job Trap

To pass along their skills to new generations and keep their trades alive, the masters of old took on apprentices who seemed to have a knack for the trade. Starting with the simplest tasks, these apprentices learned more and more parts of their trade until they eventually mastered all aspects of it.

The Industrial Revolution, in effect, put a stop to this kind of learning relationship. The master's workshop gave way to the assembly line. The apprentice was replaced by the semiskilled worker; for many, all progress toward mastery stopped after the worker learned the few basic tasks necessary to hold and perform a job.

It is these types of jobs, still with us today, that you should avoid. Just because a job exists and you can get it doesn't make taking it a smart move. Many entry-level jobs involve routine, boring, unskilled or semiskilled tasks that no one else wants to do but that are essential to the organization's functioning. This is all right—you have to learn the grunt work as well as the good stuff—but think of it as temporary. Use it as an entrée into a profession.

Before accepting an entry-level position, make sure you find out if you'll be on a professional growth track. In a bank, for instance, you may go to work as a clerk in any of several departments, such as commercial loans,

TEN FASTEST-GROWING OCCUPATIONS 1994-2005

► **Personal and home care aides**

► **Home health aides**

► **Systems analysts**

► **Computer engineers**

► **Physical and corrective therapy assistants**

► **Electronic pagination systems workers**

► **Occupational therapy assistants and aides**

► **Physical therapists**

► **Residential counselors**

► **Human services workers**

accounts receivable, or investments. If you're treated as an apprentice, you'll be given opportunities to work in different departments and learn new procedures, new policies, new skills. You may find a mentor who will watch over your shoulder and offer advice, guidance, and training in crucial areas, and who will help move you to the next level of mastery when you are ready. You may get to be a teller, a claims adjuster, and an investment officer. In a sense, you will be getting paid to learn.

Eventually, with wise tutelage, you may learn all of the principles and practices of banking. You may experience every aspect of banking and learn to make wise decisions and take appropriate actions because of your grasp of the whole, as well as your skill in working each of the tasks.

On the other hand, if your entry-level job doesn't lead to other learning and responsibilities, if you're not encouraged to learn all the basic practices surrounding the job, look elsewhere. You may spend your entire work life doing only a piece of the whole, never becoming a master of your profession. You may get good at what little you do and get high performance ratings, but you're in a dead-end job.

Gateways to Mastery

Where are the jobs that will open the doors for you? Look among the professions and organizations that are adding the most jobs. If it's a job seeker's market, you're in a better position to move around from job to job, adding new skills and competencies as you go and enhancing your experience, responsibilities, reputation, and compensation.

The Bureau of Labor Statistics has projected the ten fastest-growing occupations and the ten with the largest job growth for the years 1994 through 2005. (The fastest-growing jobs are those that are increasing in numbers over time the fastest; largest job growth are those occupations that are currently employing the most people.) Read these lists; think about each occupation listed. Which do you think are broadest and have the greatest possibility as platforms for professional learning and mastery?

This exercise is not meant to suggest that you should seek any of these jobs. The object is to see how each fits into the Web of Work. As you study the list, picture the professions, industries, and organizations involved in each occupation.

► What basic need does each occupation address?

► What entry requirements might there be?

► What growth opportunities do you see?

► Which occupations appear to be dead ends?

► Which occupations might lead to further professional development?

When you consider any job or assess any work opportunity, you will

> **TEN OCCUPATIONS WITH LARGEST JOB GROWTH 1994–2005**
>
> ► *Cashiers*
>
> ► *Janitors and cleaners, maids, household cleaners*
>
> ► *Salespersons, retail*
>
> ► *Waiters and waitresses*
>
> ► *Registered nurses*
>
> ► *General managers, top executives*
>
> ► *Systems analysts*
>
> ► *Home health aides*
>
> ► *Guards*
>
> ► *Nursing aides, orderlies, attendants*

Constructing Your Web of Work

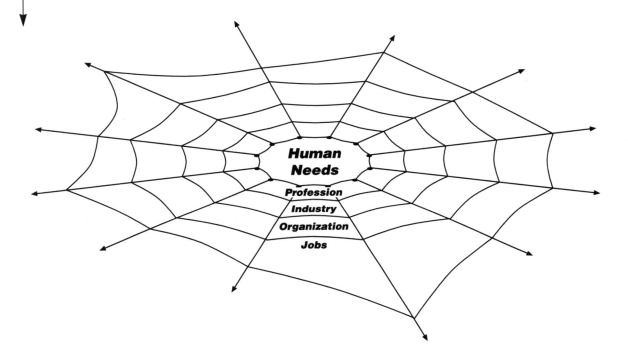

find it very instructive to draw that portion of the Web. This will help you frame the questions you need to ask to discover the long-term career opportunities as well as the short-term job prospects. What need does it serve? What profession holds the job? What industries and which organizations have these jobs?

For either the job you hold now or one you want to consider, use the diagram above and construct your own Web of Work. Write the name or type of job at the outer edge of the Web. Working toward the center of the Web, note the organizations, industries, and professions associated with that job. Note also the human need or needs the job will address.

The Amazing Disappearing Job

Millions of jobs will disappear this year, either because the conditions that once made them necessary no longer exist, or because better ways to work have been developed. Technological breakthroughs in farm machinery and pesticides have resulted in enormous increases in agricultural productivity—while drastically reducing farm jobs.

NEW WORKER

▶ *Be smart in assessing job possibilities. Always review the job in terms of how much you can learn and how easily you can move to other jobs in your profession or trade.*

▶ *Working in a smaller organization may give you more opportunities to master a wide range of professional tasks and practices. However, because you are less likely to work with a master, compensate by joining professional associations and building an outside network of support and learning.*

IN TRANSITION

▶ *If you've been outplaced, has your job disappeared or has it merely been outsourced to a company specializing in your profession? Be very careful about doing the same job again in a similar organization.*

▶ *If you have advanced to a high level of expertise in your profession, consider packaging your talents and selling them under contract to several companies.*

EXPERIENCED WORKER

▶ *You've probably experienced most of the pitfalls discussed in this chapter. You've had low-skilled jobs, jobs requiring most of your professional expertise, jobs you loved and felt good about, jobs that simply paid the bills. Now think about what you really have to offer, what you want to do—and prepare to create your own work.*

The same is true in many other manual labor jobs. In 1955, one-third of the U.S. workforce was employed in various manufacturing jobs. Forty years later that figure had fallen to 16 percent, and some economists predict that barely 12 percent of America's workers will be engaged in manufacturing by the year 2005. The reason? Increased productivity. During the 1980s, when industrial jobs underwent a steep decline, our national manufacturing productivity rose by 35 percent.[1] We are moving from brawn to brain.

Rising productivity affects us all, not just those who perform manual labor. Middle management jobs are in decline as automated control and information systems replace them and as noncore functions are contracted out to smaller, more efficient vendors. When you assess a job opportunity, pay special attention to trends in automation. Is your job likely to be replaced by a machine within the next few years? If it is, would your skills cover operating, perhaps even repairing, that machine? Will your employer give you the opportunity to add to your competencies so that you can stay ahead of the coming changes?

Your Job Audit

List three or four jobs you want to study more closely. Then answer the following questions:

- ▶ What basic needs has each one centered on?

- ▶ What professions hold each of the jobs?

- ▶ What organizations hire people to do these jobs?

- ▶ What industries need each of the jobs?

Technology, Reengineering, and Customers

14

JOBS ARE DISAPPEARING, but professions are expanding. Does this seem paradoxical? Not if you know the trends. And not if you understand the difference between a job and a profession. Computer technology, among other factors, is devouring old-style, repetitive, low-skilled jobs by the thousands. Some of these are being replaced by supervisors' jobs—supervisors of computers, that is. Other jobs are popping up in the rapidly growing service sector, where the base-level job tends to be lower paying than the manufacturing job it replaces. And still others are growing fuzzy around the edges as they overlap one another and lose their identities in teams.

Techno-Quakes Rattle the Web of Work

At the outer fringes of the Web of Work, jobs make up its most fragile, fastest-changing segment. A major change anywhere in the Web can have repercussions throughout. This is particularly true in the case of technology.

Consider, for example, the vacuum tube, a device for manipulating electrical signals. Fifty years ago, glass vacuum tubes were two-inches high. Gradually vacuum tubes were replaced by transistors, which in turn were gradually decreased in size. As they shrank, engineers began packing them together onto circuit boards, and then building them into the boards themselves to create integrated circuits. Now, these tiny "chips," made of silicon, can perform the function of millions of vacuum tubes, with much less power in a fraction of the time. The most notable byproduct of this advance is the personal computer.

But there's another device that is a result of this electronic miniaturization: the television camera. These have shrunk from the unwieldy, half-Volkswagen-sized monsters of the black-and-white '50s to color videocams that can fit into a matchbox, with high-quality lenses the size of a matchstick.

Silicon chips and miniature cameras first showed up in electronics and communications, the industries that originally felt the need for them and financed their development. But their arrival rattled the entire Web of Work. Computers, of course, have found application everywhere. The miniature camera, in the form of the endoscope, has made a particularly strong impact in health care. Now, doctors can use these devices to diagnose and treat illnesses that used to require major surgery.

The following case history describes the impact of camera miniaturization on three very different jobs in the health-care industry. I've already told the first story, of course—the women whose jobs assembling suture needle kits were phased out.

Job #1: Needle Swedger

These workers were affected in two ways. New manufacturing technology made it faster and more efficient to swedge needles and sutures mechanically rather than by hand. More important, the rise of endoscopic surgery (a direct result of the miniature camera) lessened the need for sutures. Within three years, most of the several hundred jobs disappeared. And, health and recovery rates have been enhanced dramatically.

Job #2: Surgeon

Many surgical procedures changed dramatically. A different kind of hand-eye coordination was needed. Surgeons had to learn new methods of surgery. New methods of diagnosis and new treatments became possible. Patient care changed, as did payment schedules—more outpatient surgery meant fewer hospital beds needed, and thus reduced income for hospitals. And again, health is improved.

Job #3: Marketing Manager

In the health-care products industry, marketing managers' jobs require many more competencies and a much deeper understanding of the human body and surgical procedures than ever before. Instead of simply filling orders, they have to educate surgeons on the benefits and uses of the new endoscopic devices, conduct market research to compete effectively with established medical products companies, and train salespeople in the new sales approaches.

Although it's not always obvious what impact any new development might have on any given sector, this is a good example of why you should continually scan the entire Web of Work. Changes in one industry can have profound effects in many others. Although only one of these three jobs disappeared, this extinction affected hundreds of people and their families. Had they been alert to breakthroughs in the surgical and electronics industries, they would have had three years to develop new skills and find work in other parts of the company or industry. As it was, most needle swedgers were outplaced with only a few months' notice, and few of the women were prepared.

Reinventing Jobs Strengthens the Web of Work

Technology doesn't always threaten your job; used judiciously, it can improve your working conditions and make you more productive. At a Toyota RV plant in Japan, workers were invited to redesign their jobs and employ machines to make their jobs easier. With 66 percent less automation than a standard assembly line, the new assembly procedure uses a line subdivided into five parts with buffer zones to reduce stress, conveyor belts for workers to stand on that move with the vehicle, and devices to roll engines and gearboxes into place. Machines do only what the workers don't want to do. Movements are smooth and harmonious. These improvements have increased productivity by 20 percent and reduced defects by 88 percent. The efficiency is twice that of a typical American plant.[1]

No More Job Titles

"Physicians Sales and Service, projected to have 1995 sales of $235 million, shares ownership and decision making with employees. . . . Each service center was divided into teams and employees are to make whatever decisions they think are needed to keep customers happy, with or without approval by their team leaders. There are no job titles—people are expected to do whatever is needed to help customers—and pay is based on ability."[2]

Notice the part that organizational values played in this use of technology. Instead of simply replacing every worker who could be replaced by a machine, the employer asked the workers to help redesign the process, thus valuing workers over technology, empowerment over command, experiment over dogma, personnel over profit. The result was a boon not only to the workers but also to the organization. Workers developed new competencies: designing work flow, customizing machine processes, team building, and computer literacy. The organization improved efficiency and productivity, increased profits, and probably cut health-care costs and other overhead. If you were looking for a manual-labor job with a future, you couldn't do much better than an organization like this.

It's important, of course, that technological changes be used and not avoided. People who are aware of the need to improve efficiency and productivity learn to use new hardware and software to do their jobs better than ever before; those who don't often discover that the technology alone can do their jobs adequately and more cheaply.

Reengineering Rescues Professions

The restructuring of work processes for greater efficiency and productivity demonstrates why capitalism has outlived all other major economic systems. Every day we see new experiments with work structures—centralized, decentralized, teams, regions, departments, core processes, outsourcing, batching.

One major workplace trend is the increasing use of self-managed work teams, temporary groupings of individuals with specialized knowledge and skills. In such teams, everyone has the same "job"—producing a collective result. Team members use their individual strengths, thus compensating for other members' weaknesses; decisions are made by consensus of those who know the most about the problems to be solved. (*Teamsmart*™, our self-directed approach to team competencies, let's you easily assess your strengths and liabilities in any team.)

If you equate your career with a particular job title, you may feel insecure with the team concept. After all, like fences, job boundaries keep others from coming in and taking parts of your job, don't they? Perhaps, but remember—they also keep you from exploring and learning new tasks, new skills, new ways of working. And these are the things you will need to compete and survive in the workplace of the future. Keep a profession-centered mindset and choose or redesign jobs that support mastering your profession.

Examples of how work is being reorganized are all around us. Aer Lingus, Ireland's airline, decided in 1993 that it needed to speed up its engineering and maintenance functions. These functions employed fifteen hundred workers in eleven trades, each with narrowly defined tasks that no other trade was allowed to perform. When projects were handed from one trade to another, the result was serious scheduling inefficiencies.

Aer Lingus decided on a radical work restructuring. It combined the eleven trades into two major groups. With the agreement of labor, workers in eight of the trades were reclassified as mechanical engineers; those from the other three trades became avionics engineers. This was done through cross-training.

The result was hailed by all sides as a great success. Simplifying and reorganizing the tasks reduced the duplication of effort, increased both the speed and the quality of work, and created new jobs. Aer Lingus doubled its capacity for overhauling its Boeing 747s, and the workforce added seven hundred new workers.[3]

As at Aer Lingus, reengineering often consists of putting tasks back together into total processes, or total professions. Instead of having each worker perform a narrow task during a brief segment of a project, teams allow workers to use a broader set of skills and stay involved until the project is completed. Thus, reuniting processes also reunites skills—puts professions back together. The blurring of job boundaries back into professional processes is good for work and good for workers.

Serving Customer Needs

The blurring of job boundaries can also be attributed to the growth of service industries and increased attention to customer service in all industries. Not only is your job definition broadened to include occasional customer contact, but the increased authority makes you a better professional.

▶ Your empowerment as a field-level worker gives you both more responsibility and more authority to serve customers. With your desktop computer and new communications capabilities, you have more access to information than ever before. If the customer has a question, you can find the answer quickly without calling upstairs. You are encouraged to find or invent ways to get things done without fear of penalty.

▶ As a professional, you're expected to continually add to your competencies—to step outside a narrow range of activities and take part in more aspects of the business. It no longer matters as much whether you're a systems engineer, an accountant, or a customer service representative. With the increased emphasis on service in all organizations, you're expected to deal with customers whether the issue involves your specialty or not.

The new emphasis on customer service is another way that the system of work is reverting to older values. After all, the entire Web of Work has grown in size and complexity to serve basic human needs that will never disappear—and how better to stay in touch with those needs than by dealing directly with the customer at all levels? Customers' opinions and desires are now sought at the service counter, in distribution, in product improvement projects, in new-product development, in advertising, in pricing. The competition for the hearts and minds of customers grows more intense every year, and woe unto organizations or workers that fall behind.

Working Double Time

Building mastery takes time. You need a variety of jobs with different tasks to master a range of skills and competencies in a profession. You need time in each job to create a record of significant accomplishment that will carry you to your next work situation.

But in a job, time is something you can't necessarily count on—so you may have to work your job on two time scales. In the short run, you must demonstrate proficient, reliable performance and produce results in your current areas of responsibility. At the same time, you should use your job as a vehicle for acquiring new abilities and strategically position yourself for the future. Showcase your present capabilities while building new competencies for professional growth: that's how to get double value from your work time.

Meaghan currently holds a job as a sales administrator in our company. She answers customer inquiries, takes orders, tracks sales, projects client opportunities, schedules seminars, and manages the logistics of showcases. She spends much of her time working with the computer and has access to several graphic design software packages. Meaghan hasn't chosen a profession yet, but she's quite intrigued with graphic design and is always seeking opportunities to create brochures, letterhead, and unique promotional materials. She's working double time—performing her job while also enhancing her skills and the company, through creative graphics. Her supervisor recognizes the double value and looks for opportunities that benefit Meaghan, customers, and the bottom line.

Few traditional jobs are designed with this dual perspective in mind. In fact, most jobs focus exclusively on short-term requirements, matching immediate services to present needs. A few positions, such as R&D management, are specifically responsible for keeping an eye on the future. The vast majority of jobs, however, offer little incentive for taking the long view. The good news is that if you are willing to seize the initiative, most jobs can be enriched with the qualities necessary to build a rewarding career over time.

Which qualities are those? Recall what I said earlier about the three benefits of work. Truly rewarding work often provides a livelihood—a way

NEW WORKER

► *Wherever you are working or looking for work, ask people about the trends they see in their jobs. Pay particular attention to the eight indicators of job vitality (discussed further in the next chapter).*

► *Find out the impact of technology on the job as well as on the organization. What is the longevity of the job? What is the learning potential?*

IN TRANSITION

► *Has technology affected your past and current jobs positively or negatively?*

► *How will the next job you are considering be affected by technology? Will it be enhanced or will it disappear?*

EXPERIENCED WORKER

► *How has technology affected your past and current jobs, both positively and negatively?*

► *Are you skilled in using computers and other technologies?*

► *How can you harness technology to create the kind of work you want in the future?*

to attain economic security, however ambitious or modest your goals. Work can also be a source of continuous growth and learning. Finally, your work can add meaning to your life by repaying the devotion of your efforts with a deep conviction that your time has been well spent. If you find these attributes in your work, then your job title and position on the organizational totem pole are largely irrelevant. If they are absent, your job will probably seem frustrating and oppressive, no matter what position you hold.

Consider your present or most recent job. How does it measure up to these important characteristics of rewarding work?

- ► Does your job offer opportunities for attaining your financial goals?

- ► Do you learn new skills and competencies in the normal course of your job?

- ► Does your job provide opportunities to develop the skills and competencies that will be crucial for the future of your industry, your profession, and your career?

- ► How would you change your job to make your work more meaningful and satisfying?

It is crucial to maintain a clear mental distinction between your present job, which belongs to the organization, and your profession—your portfolio of marketable career skills. No job by itself can be a solid foundation for career stability; it is simply a way to package your unique skills, talents, and competencies and negotiate compensation. Jobs in their traditional form (routine tasks, finite pieces of whole professions) are on their way out, but many new ways of packaging and combining skills, both by the individual and by teams, will be explored in the decades to come, and the customer's needs—the basic human needs—will always be at the stable center of the Web of Work.

Characteristics of Great Jobs

*I*N AN IDEAL WORLD, what should you expect from a job? Satisfaction, economic reward, opportunities to grow, of course. It would also be nice if you could *keep* your ideal job long enough to take a full measure of its benefits. But how likely is that in today's rapidly changing world of work?

You can't predict how long you'll be working where you are, so it makes sense to choose jobs that will continue to be in demand in other places. Match your current job, or a job you are considering, against the indicators of job vitality listed below. If it fails to meet four or more of the criteria, your job is at risk.

Crucial Delivery of the Organization's Mission

Every organization has work to perform, without which it could not accomplish its fundamental purpose. People who can deliver this core work are essential to the organization's success. Jobs that are essential to the mission of the organization—doctors and nurses in a hospital, firefighters in a fire department—are more likely to survive periods of upheaval and change. Jobs that facilitate the organization's mission but are not directly engaged in its core work—staffing personnel in a hospital, cleaners in a fire department—are at greater risk.

When the organization is under pressure to streamline, the quick fix is to eliminate secondary jobs. This is why many of the positions now being lost in downsizing are administrative or managerial. Although they provide valuable support and coordination, they are not essential to the mission. The more directly your work contributes to the bottom line, the stronger your position. Consider the following questions about whether your job is essential:

> **EIGHT INDICATORS OF JOB VITALITY**
>
> 1. **Crucial to organization mission**
> 2. **Enhances and requires mastery**
> 3. **Close to the customer**
> 4. **Creates visibility in the profession**
> 5. **Growth options in industry**
> 6. **Longevity**
> 7. **Fits values and interests**
> 8. **Provides a service to others**

▶ Does your current job directly support the organization's mission?

▶ What value does your job add to the organization?

▶ What specific organization strategies require your skills and the value you deliver in your current job?

▶ Does your job contribute directly to the bottom line? How?

Seek Jobs that Enhance and Require Mastery

Work that requires a high degree of specialization and proficiency is comparatively stable, particularly if the specialty is essential to the organization's purpose. Master practitioners in any field are not easily replaced. Expert knowledge and demonstrated proficiency command respect.

A potential hazard of practicing your specialty in a single job over a long time, however, is the risk of falling behind the state of the art in your profession. Specialties take years to master but can quickly lose their market value. It is wise to balance your expertise in a specific area of work by keeping up to date with the broader industry and profession. Continual, lifelong learning in your chosen field is more than a lofty ideal—it's a practical and necessary investment in your own future, a hedge against the inevitable day when your specialty is transformed by new developments.

Think about the following points when evaluating your job's learning requirements:

▶ How can you easily expand your professional skill set in your current job?

▶ What new competencies or practices will the job require you to learn?

▶ What developmental assignments or experiences could you incorporate into your job to increase your level of expertise?

▶ How well do the job requirements accommodate the next steps you must take to enhance your professional skills?

▶ Will mentors be easy to find? How? Where?

Stay Close to the Customer

Look for jobs that are close to the customer. Taking care of customers and constituents is an essential function of any organization, from government agency to corner convenience store. Customers can expand your visibility and contacts with other people and organizations, and they can provide another perspective on your industry. Customer needs are usually a more dependable source of work than are an organization's internal routines. Front-line jobs responding directly to customer needs are on the increase, while "back room" jobs (including many managerial positions) are being cut.

Keep a watchful eye on the technological horizon, though. Bank tellers and gas station attendants work close to their customers, but their jobs are swiftly becoming obsolete because of ATMs and self-service pumps. The overall workplace trend is to automate any customer service function that does not require expert technical knowledge or personal hospitality.

How close to the customer is your job or the job you are interested in? Ask yourself these questions:

▶ How does my work help my customers?

▶ Who or what could replace my services?

▶ What other services could I provide to bring me more directly into contact with customers?

▶ How could I make my contributions more visible to people inside and outside my organization?

Maintain Visibility in Your Profession

To become a master in your profession, you must learn. To learn, you must surround yourself with masters and mentors. This may be hard to do, especially in a small organization, but you can't learn everything you need to know on your own. Unless the organization is diligent in providing you a mentor or expert colleagues, it's up to you to make yourself more visible and find mentors.

Early in your career, seek out a job that lets you learn from and compete with your professional peers. Look for an organization known for excellence and for grooming and supporting new workers. Choose a job where being visible to others in the organization and the industry is a natural part of your work. Build a strong professional support network. Don't get stuck in a back room, especially if your job keeps you so busy you don't have time to learn new competencies or keep up with the trends in your industry and profession.

The following questions will help you assess the visibility of your job:

▶ Who sees your work and can give you quality feedback?

▶ What kind of interaction do you have with others in your profession?

▶ Will your work necessitate becoming visible outside the organization? to whom?

▶ With whom will you be working most of the time? What are their skill levels? What exposure will they foster for you?

Pursue Personal Growth Options in the Industry

The world of work has its fads and fashions. Specific skills are subject to periods of intense demand, followed by periods of diminished interest. In the 1970s there was a public outcry because of a perceived shortage of college students enrolling in engineering programs. But as a result of the loss of key industries to foreign competition and the downsizing of our national defense industry, unemployed engineers now glut the market in some regions.

What at first seemed to be isolated problems in a few companies soon turned out to be widespread problems that threatened the existence of entire domestic industries such as the automobile, steel, and consumer electronics industries. Like canaries in a coal mine, the early failures and layoffs in those industries warned of calamitous events to come.

It pays to be constantly attentive to the latest industry developments. If the demand for the job you do is not growing in your industry, jobs may start declining. The time to start thinking about switching industries or learning new skills is when the first signs of decline emerge, not after they are in full swing.

Here's how to assess your job's growth opportunities in your industry:

► What are the hiring and downsizing patterns for people in your job? in your industry?

► Are your competitors expanding their business in the areas requiring your skills, or are they cutting back?

► Are there many start-up ventures in your industry that are developing new niches related to your job?

► What trends can you detect in professional journals, industry newsletters, and Internet news groups in your profession?

Create Longevity

Besides asking whether the demand for your work is declining or growing, try to anticipate how long it will be performed. Thirty years ago, becoming an auto mechanic meant acquiring a body of knowledge and manual skills, some self-taught, others learned under the supervision of an experienced teacher. But today's cars are so complex that mechanics must be able to analyze computer diagnostics, service elaborate electronic systems, and decipher repair manuals from half a dozen countries.

A mechanic in the 1990s requires a whole new set of tools, both physical and conceptual, to master the craft. The same is true in virtually every profession. Advances in technology are changing the way we all work. Innovations such as telecommuting and teleconferencing give rise to new ways of working. "Virtual organizations" electronically link the experts needed to perform a specific task without the associated costs of a shared physical location or a full-time work group.

How long will your job endure? The following questions may help you decide:

▶ How will your work be performed three, five, or ten years from now?

▶ What new developments can you anticipate that will change your work practices and relationships?

▶ What do you need to start doing today to prepare yourself for that future?

▶ Whom can you talk with to explore new competencies and skill sets that will be needed?

Is the Job a Good Fit?

Sometimes you take a job to meet needs in other parts of your life—for instance, a job that's not in your profession but that is close to home, that leaves you plenty of time for your family, or that pays enough to support you while you pursue your real career interest, playing drums in a rock band.

Ideally, you will find a job that satisfies all your life requirements and your professional goals as well—a job that fits you at many levels. Aim high—look for a job that fits your interests, passions, professional development, personality, and personal mission. Find work that lets you be uniquely yourself in the fullest sense. You'll stay healthier, happier, and more productive.

How healthy and happy does your job keep you?

▶ In what ways does the job allow and encourage you to use your talents?

▶ How well does the job fit your aspirations and goals?

▶ Which of your needs does the job satisfy?

Offer a Service to Others

The most fulfilling aspect of work for many people is providing a service to others. Directly or indirectly, your job helps many people take care of their human needs. The more you see how your work enriches others, the greater your sense of contribution.

Strive to find a job that keeps you in close contact with people, that lets you connect directly with their needs. For most people, being engaged physically, emotionally, and intellectually with others is more fulfilling than working as a hermit. Thinking of your work as a service helps you go the extra mile toward mastering your profession.

Ask yourself these questions about your job and its contribution to others:

▶ What services does my job provide? to whom?

▶ Who would be in trouble if my job did not exist or if I didn't perform it competently?

▶ How does service relate to income? to profitability?

▶ Does my work take care of one of the human needs I care about?

PART VII

Weaving Your Own
Web of Work

"There is only one success—
to be able to spend life your own way."

—*Christopher Morley*

You've seen how trends that start anywhere in the Web of Work can ripple through the entire Web and change, or even eliminate, your job or organization. Although the human need that calls for your work will always be there, the way it is addressed keeps changing. Change brings uncertainty, and it often seems that you're not in control of your work life.

But change also brings opportunity. Technological, economic, and societal trends create new ways of working. The way you work, where you work—indeed, the very nature of work itself—is changing dramatically. The marketplace is becoming more sophisticated and demanding new ways of delivering traditional products and services, not to mention the flood of new ones that seem to appear almost daily. Change creates openings in the Web of Work that can be filled by your unique services. If you can see these changing patterns, you can jump in and fill them in a uniquely valuable way.

And you can do more than fulfill the needs of an employer. In these times when the entire concept of work is changing, you can shape your work life in more ways than ever before. You can package your skills and competencies in a variety of ways that not only meet your customer's needs but also suit your personal and professional lifestyle. And by using your innate talents to create new products or new services, you will gain professional stability.

How do you do this? By thinking like an entrepreneur. By changing the

NEW WORKER

▶ *Hook up with a couple of friends and brainstorm through this section together.*

▶ *Follow your natural instincts; dream up wonderful new products and services that give people what they need.*

▶ *Compare what you love to do with what others need.*

IN TRANSITION

▶ *Use this opportunity to craft your work setting, style, and role according to your self-assessment and personal requirements.*

▶ *Don't rush to take a full-time job; shop the options and craft your own work contract.*

▶ *Put much more emphasis on what you have to offer than on what you want to get.*

EXPERIENCED WORKER

▶ *If you've mastered your profession, you can probably name your perfect work setting and compensation package.*

▶ *Look ahead; feel the tremors and changes in the Web of Work. Help prepare your organization and your customers for new ways of doing things.*

▶ *Keep your profession moving with the times. Be a mentor for new professionals.*

way you view work. Not by looking for a job, but by creating work. *By asking, "What do I have to offer that will help this situation or person?" By designing your own means of fulfilling that need. And that's what this section is about.*

Having constructed your own mental map of the ever-changing Web of Work, you now have a new vantage point from which to design your career. You can survey what's happening throughout the Web and, moving grace-

fully into and out of industries, organi-zations, and jobs that fit you, you can master the skills involved in taking care of human needs.

This section will show you several ways to package your talents and offer your services to customers—those who will pay you for the benefits of your

skills and competencies. You will com-plete a Capability Portfolio and, in the process, find that you have many more options than you might have thought for finding or creating rewarding work. You will discover that you can be in control of your career—and it will give you new confidence.

Creating Your Work Niche

*Which Roles
Do You Play
Best?*

*Work
Environment:
Capability
and Comfort*

*T*ODAY'S EXCITING TRENDS will open many more doors than they close. They herald self-sufficiency, encourage us to create new ways of working, and enable us to match our working options with our basic needs. The growing power of the electronic network is finally letting us realize the concept of the global village. People will now be able to go back to their communities, stay close to home, and still work and contribute to the global community. Of course, computer skills are a must for opening these doors.

Changes in our work landscape are numerous and reveal many niches:

▶ Small businesses (fewer than one hundred employees) account for 70 percent of our economic growth.

▶ Firms with fewer than twenty employees have added 4.4 million new jobs in the past four years.

▶ The ranks of the self-employed are increasing dramatically. Today, more than 45 million people in the United States are self-employed, temporary workers, part-timers, consultants, or job sharers.

▶ Temporary services companies are a booming industry and now supply the entire range of employment resources, including accountants, executives, programmers, system designers, project managers, nurses, hospice workers, technical consultants, and graphic designers.

This chapter will help you package your skills to take advantage of these trends while assuring that your personal needs are met. It will also help you assess several different packaging options in the context of the environmental factors or values that are most important to you.[1] There are two steps:

▶ First, determine what service roles you play best: resource provider, project manager, specialist, or strategist. All four are needed in our flowering economy. You may find one role that best captures a way to speak about your special service. The following self-assessment exercise may show you powerful new ways to think about and package your capabilities.

▶ Second, reevaluate your work environment. For personal and professional reasons, these factors change throughout your lifetime. Knowing which ones are most important to you now and which ones provide harmony between your personal and professional life enables you to negotiate working conditions that suit your needs—conditions you should be reluctant to compromise.

The next chapter will also help you explore five alternative work contracts beyond full-time employment. You can study each, evaluate which works best for you, and prepare to restructure your work life accordingly.

Which Roles Do You Play Best?

In the future, you and others will think of your work more in terms of the service you provide than the position you hold. As organizations get smaller, team up, build alliances and partnerships, and get closer to the customer, these services will be defined in terms of four fundamental roles.

Following are questions that will help you think of yourself as a service provider rather than a job holder. This questionnaire is designed to help you distinguish the different service roles and craft future work assignments and projects that maximize them.[2] Read the description of each role and see if it aligns with your prior experience. Think especially of the times when you were happiest and felt most successful in your work or life. Place a check mark beside each statement you think is true. Six or more marks suggests that you are strong in that role.

Project managers excel in managing complex interdisciplinary teams, on time, on budget, with accomplished teammates and satisfied customers. They enjoy coordinating, managing, scheduling, and organizing the many people and activities needed to complete a project successfully. They can see the big picture and the little pieces simultaneously.

- [ ] You're skilled at choreographing complex projects or events.
- [ ] You're a natural organizer.
- [ ] You're good at managing multiple time and delivery schedules.
- [ ] You're able to anticipate and avoid potential breakdowns before they happen and motivate people to correct them.
- [ ] You're a natural team builder and motivator. People love to work with you.
- [ ] You have highly developed people skills.
- [ ] You would rather orchestrate work than do the work.
- [ ] You thrive on interpersonal and team challenges.
- [ ] You have a reputation for accomplishment, bringing projects in on time, on budget, with satisfied customers.
- [ ] You attract and keep talented people for projects.

Resource providers link people and information with organizations and industries. More and more information is stored in open databases. More and more people are leaving large organizations to work for themselves. As these information and people resources grow, resource providers broker individual services to clients and help organizations find the resources and information they need.

- [ ] You enjoy and excel at matching needs with resources.
- [ ] You're comfortable and proficient with the use of various information systems technologies.
- [ ] You enjoy being a matchmaker for people and resources.
- [ ] You have a competency mindset, easily seeing people's talent.
- [ ] You enjoy making deals, both internally and externally, to provide resources.
- [ ] You have a broad network of aligned professionals and companies and can put together virtual teams easily and productively.

☐ You can use information systems technology effectively in your work.

☐ You can match talent with the demands of internal and external customers.

☐ You know how the business works and which resources count for success.

☐ You negotiate "smart" projects—innovative, cost-effective, leveraging talent, and so on.

Specialists have deep, broad expertise in one or more professions, crafts, or trades. They assure quality, service, and state-of-the-art craftsmanship for organizations and industries. They can counsel, advise, consult, or be members of interdisciplinary teams developing new products or services. They can work closely with customers to define and satisfy their needs.

☐ You love the challenges of a particular profession or discipline.

☐ You are a self-starting learner, staying at the leading edge of your professional discipline.

☐ You have passion for work and the services you can provide in your profession.

☐ You successfully take on more and more complex projects in your profession.

☐ You identify with and have first loyalty to your profession.

☐ You seek breadth and depth in your area of specialization.

☐ You are sought out by others in your profession for your savvy and experience.

☐ Your reputation in professional circles is as one of the best in your profession.

☐ You see yourself as a specialist rather than a generalist.

☐ You are sought after as a mentor and coach in your profession.

Strategists are the intellectual leaders and visionaries who pave the way for breakthroughs in a profession, industry, or organization. They create new niches and expand existing ones. They have a long-term, strategic view.

- ☐ You've worked in the industry or organization long enough to be a leader.
- ☐ You habitually take a systems viewpoint in solving problems.
- ☐ You have mastered one or more of the core professions in your industry or organization.
- ☐ You have strong connections and alliances throughout the industry.
- ☐ You are passionate about redesigning the industry.
- ☐ You are more interested in what happens ten years from now than in the next quarter.
- ☐ You can participate in high-level discussions in the core technologies.
- ☐ You are often consulted by industry colleagues for your know-how.
- ☐ You are consulted regarding problems and trends in the industry.
- ☐ You are committed to excellence in addressing industry trends and problems.

Your totals should give you a sense of the role/roles you see yourself in and where to focus your attention. Scores that are fairly close together suggest that you may, more easily than most, move between the roles according to your circumstances, opportunities, and preferences.

According to Thomas Stewart, companies will need the following approximate balance of roles in the immediate future:

- ▶ 60–70 percent specialists
- ▶ 10 percent strategists
- ▶ 5–10 percent resource providers
- ▶ 15–20 percent project managers.[3]

Some people will be able to move comfortably between two roles. Others will design their careers to excel in only one role; they will find or design niches where their service is required and where they can be a preferred provider. Given your preferred role or roles, you can craft experiences and build relationships that will open up those niches.

Work Environment: Capability and Comfort

We've talked elsewhere about the importance of personal values, organization culture, and the importance of "fit." When the work setting is in harmony with your values and preferred style of work, you are happier, more efficient, and more productive. In the past, most of us had little control over where we worked and could do little to shape our environment once we got there. Today, however, choosing or crafting a work setting that suits you is an important part of running your own career. Your comfort level in a work setting depends on a variety of cultural factors—informality, friendliness, pace, flexibility, and others—that differ widely among organizations. You should become an expert at searching out these factors and assessing not only whether you can do the work but whether you will like it.

Once you've decided which environmental factors are most important, you can assess your current or future niches in light of them. This cultural fit is essential for people who are already mature professionals. The older and more talented you are, the more important the harmony between your personal values and the organization's cultural values. You need to work in places and situations that don't go against your grain if you are truly to make a contribution and feel proud of your work.

What Do You Value at Work?

Following are listed cultural factors that you will find in different work environments. Read through the list and rank them as follows: M = must have; N = nice to have; D = don't care. Choose the seven that are most important to you. Feel free to add other factors you know to be important.

___ **Access to experts in profession**

___ **Camaraderie, friendliness**

___ **Challenging work**

___ **Child care or elder care**

___ **Competitive pay and benefits**

___ **Diversity valued**

___ **Educational benefits**

___ **Employee ownership options**

___ **Familial feeling**

___ **Flexible work schedules**

___ **Innovation valued**

___ **Minimal travel**

___ **Openness, trust**

___ **Participation in decision making**

___ **Pension plan, profit sharing**

___ **Pride in work**

___ **Product or service contributes to society**

___ **Productivity tools, connectivity**

___ **Reputation in industry**

___ **Sabbaticals**

___ **Teamwork**

___ **Telecommuting accepted**

___ **Working at home**

NEW WORKER

▶ *If you're working, assess your business environment. Use drinking fountains, cafeterias, and elevators as opportunities for small talk. Ask lots of "dumb" questions—what's really important around here? How do you get in trouble?*

▶ *If you're looking for work or trying to decide whom to work with, ask specific questions and keep your eyes open when you interview.*

IN TRANSITION

▶ *If you're checking out other organizations, design a list of interview questions to check for your preferred cultural factors.*

▶ *Don't ask just your interviewers; ask people who have no reason, conscious or unconscious, to influence you. One of the best places to do this is in the cafeteria. Strike up conversations with several people who work there.*

▶ *Read industry reports on prospective employers. What's their reputation?*

▶ *Open your eyes and look around.*

EXPERIENCED WORKER

▶ *Think about your current and past work environments. Where were you most productive? Where were you happiest? Are those places the same?*

▶ *Which environmental factors are most important to you at this stage in your career?*

▶ *If you are working, test for ways to meet your environmental concerns. You may feel inclined to look elsewhere for a better fit, but don't give up prematurely on your current work situation.*

Working on Your Own Terms

*I*N A VIRTUAL WORK WORLD with real-time global connections, people have work options that didn't even exist five years ago. With organizations tightening their belts and keeping only core professionals, the contingent workforce grows daily. Over 45 million people, 33 percent of employed adults, do some work from home, up from 27 million five years ago. Telecommuters numbered over 8 million in 1996 and are projected to exceed 12 million in 1997.[1]

Contingent Workforce

More than one-third of the American workforce is either self-employed or working as temps, part-timers, or consultants. This so-called contingent workforce has grown 57 percent since 1980, three times faster than the labor force as a whole.[2]

There are many exciting ways to package your work, to market the product that is you. If you're working for others, you can take care of your personal and professional needs while giving top value to your employer. Or you can start your own business or join others in a start-up activity.

In every packaging option there are pros and cons that change over time. At some phases in your professional and personal life, you enjoy stress—you like challenging work, big projects, long hours, a sense of accomplishing great things. In other periods you need more time for family, friends, vacations, relaxation, and contemplation. You can now design cycles of high stress and low stress into your life by taking sabbaticals, working at home by yourself, or working remotely with others online.

Besides full-time employment, the most frequently used packaging options are

> ► temporary work

> ► freelance, consulting, or contract work

> ► part-time work or job sharing

> ► telecommuting

> ► starting your own business

Read through the descriptions and examples of each packaging option, then see which ones are most appealing to you. Fill in the matrix below as you read about each option. Determine which options fulfill most of your work environment values. This knowledge will be crucial in negotiating your current and future work situations.

Temporary Work

As permanent jobs grow more scarce, temporary employees pick up more of the work. "Temps," people who are called in as needed for special projects, jobs, or services, are on the increase in most industries and professions. CEOs from Fortune 500 firms have said they expect to rely more and more on temporary staff rather than adding to their permanent payrolls. Talent is being seen more as a commodity to be purchased, used, and replaced as needed, and the growing variety of temporary services available makes it easier to think this way.[3]

Not so long ago, "temps" meant clerical or administrative workers, like Kelly Girls. Today you can find temp agencies and temp workers in almost every professional field—financial consulting, environmental science, programming, human resources, manufacturing, fund-raising, accounting, materials management, sales, marketing, administrative services, architecture, engineering, and on and on.[4] One of the fastest growing segments is the hiring and placing of top managers—about 20 percent of all professionals work as temps.[5]

The growth and diversification of temp agencies, the rising cost of health care and other employee benefits, and the survival imperative to "do more with less" combine to make temping an attractive option for both organizations and individuals. The number of temporary placement companies will grow even faster if mandatory company-paid health insurance is approved by Congress in coming years.

> ### GOOD NEWS!
>
> *Competent knowledge workers—people working with information and ideas—can truly name their game and their price if, and only if, they know how valuable they are and to whom.*

Temporary work is often a temporary situation—a way for you to move from an unsatisfactory career position into a work environment that suits you better. As you build a reputation with temp agencies, you move onto a special list, giving you and the agency the ability to collaborate effectively, especially for key clients. The contacts you make can lead you to other kinds of work opportunities, such as part-time or full-time work or self-employment.

The Strategy of Temporary Work

"Temping" makes sense in a variety of situations:

As a stepping-stone into work. While studying, during summer vacation, or upon graduation, many college or high school students sign up with temporary agencies to build their résumé, get work experience in a variety of industries, and learn what kind of organization they fit best in.

As a transitional step back into the workforce. People who have left or lost full-time employment often find it easier to get back to work by temping. Jobs that take only one or two days, for example, leave the rest of the week open for learning new skills, considering new professions, and interviewing with other employers under less-than-emergency conditions.

As a supplement to another's income. Not *having* to work gives you more freedom. Although you're on call, you can gracefully decline. You can choose when, where, and what to do, building your experience, skills, and reputation under carefully controlled circumstances.

As an entrée into full-time work. Although returning to permanent employment happens less and less frequently, sometimes part-timers do such an outstanding job that bringing them on board full-time is a risk-free and attractive option for the employer.

Ask yourself these questions:

> ▶ What do I consider the pros and cons of temping?

> ▶ In which areas could I see myself temping?

► Do I know someone I can talk to who has done temporary work?

► Which local temporary agencies employ people in my profession?

Freelance, Consulting, or Contract Work

More and more self-employed professionals are running their own one-person shows, contracting by the job or project to a variety of client organizations. Highly paid specialists—engineers, chemists, project managers—who used to work for one company until retirement are joining the ranks of traditional freelancers such as writers, illustrators, lawyers, accountants, and physicians.

This is a situation in which everyone benefits. Professionals can specialize in their expertise and follow their passion. What's more, their work increases in value with the depth and breadth of the experience they gain from a variety of assignments. Organizations that contract for their work do not have to pay for their health insurance, vacation time, pensions, profit-sharing plans, or other overhead.

The rapid growth of information and communication technologies not only lets people accomplish more on their own, it also makes it easier for the vendor to find business opportunities and for the company to locate service providers. Even a casual contact can lead to freelance consulting work. Our firm recently replied to a piece of misrouted e-mail and ended up talking with a university professor who was also a consultant in a field in which we sometimes need expert help. By accident, he gained a potential client.

To concentrate on their specialties, freelancers sometimes refer overflow work to one another and contract out for more general or "housekeeping" services. The result is the spontaneous creation of a new kind of

TEMPS

In 1994, nearly 2 million people worked in temporary jobs on an average day—up 28 percent from the year before.

—Bureau of Labor Statistics of the U.S. Department of Labor, February 1995.

organization, a loose, informal group of associates called a "virtual corporation." Loose confederations of self-employed workers offer the advantages of a ready-made team to work on a specific engineering or other problem. In Toronto, four freelance engineers using Lotus Notes have formed a loose, company-like framework for about 150 independent consultants. Working teams form and dissolve according to clients' needs. Associates, who remain self-employed, pay a fee to join the network and gain access to its special services. In return, the company provides group discounts on insurance, long-distance telephone service, and access to databases and job banks.

Why Freelance or Do Contract Work?

At times in your career, you may find freelancing the best way to package your competencies for any of several reasons:

To broaden your experience. You may have spent most of your working life in one industry or even one company. Freelancing lets you explore other industries and organizations. You can expand your support network and business alliances and gain access to new information and technology.

To test an idea for a small business. If you can freelance while you're fully employed—that is, moonlight—you can test-market your services, work out the bugs, and round up a few clients. Then, when you are ready, you can cut the ties and put all your time and energy into developing your new business.

To become a specialist rather than a generalist. Consulting in a niche lets you develop depth and mastery in one area. Operating a small business often means, at least initially, accepting a lot of work that doesn't interest you. But as your reputation grows, you can concentrate on the kinds of work you like and perform best and develop a clientele requiring that product or service.

To practice your passion.   Sometimes you can't make enough money to support yourself with work that satisfies your true passion, but you can make a contribution to others and begin gaining recognition. Some people offer part-time art and music services to schools or to students; cooking for a hobby can produce satisfaction and a small following.

Ask yourself the following questions:

▶ What advantages or disadvantages are there in being a freelance consultant?

▶ What conditions would have to exist for me to freelance?

▶ What capability or competency do I have that makes me confident others would pay for my services?

▶ How many freelance consultants do I know? Who could I talk to?

▶ Which aspects of my personality lend themselves to free-lancing? Which aspects may work against it?

Part-Time Work and Job Sharing

In today's workplace it's sometimes easier to find one or two part-time jobs than one full-time job. Many companies are allowing workers to share jobs—to split duties, responsibilities, and compensation fifty-fifty or other-wise. They have found this a good way to keep competent people who

PART-TIMERS

Four million professionals worked part-time in 1995. This includes attorneys, computer specialists, scientists, and engineers.

—Bureau of Labor Statistics of the U.S. Department of Labor, 1995

prefer to split their time between part-time work and family responsibilities or between different kinds of work. In many cases, work slots can be redesigned to reduce down time and increase productivity.

Employers have discovered that many kinds of work lend themselves well to part-time or split positions. Some projects can be easily divided into discrete jobs or tasks among several professionals—retail sales, computer repair and troubleshooting, market research, graphic design, and word processing are examples. Some work is so stressful that long hours are undesirable; social services casework, emergency service dispatch, and air traffic control come to mind. Other tasks simply don't require full-time staffing or can be completed in a day or less. Still other jobs are not time-sensitive and can be done by persons working at unconventional hours.

Part-time and job-sharing work used to be confined to skilled service providers in the lower levels of certain kinds of organizations. Today you can find examples from top to bottom in all professions and trades:

▶ NBC News has had two working-mother reporters, Victoria Corderi and Lisa Rudolph, sharing the correspondent role for *Now* and *Dateline NBC.*

▶ Texas Instruments split its CEO position between two senior executives and two senior executive positions among four vice presidents.

▶ First National Bank of Chicago had two working mothers sharing the presidency, supervising eighteen employees and overseeing $35 million in deposits, by working three days each, one of them together.

Why Job-Share or Work Part-Time?

Job sharing or part-time work may make a lot of sense if you are

a single parent or one-half of a two-career couple who needs to balance work with parenting, taking care of an elderly parent, or meeting community responsibilities.

a dedicated professional who wishes to learn new skills, continue your formal education, establish a reputation in more than one organization at a time, or make a gradual transition to a new job or profession.

a high achiever who can live comfortably on earnings from part-time work while moving into a lower gear to reduce stress in your life.

Ask yourself the following:

▶ What job-sharing opportunities are there in my profession?

▶ What are the pros and cons of job sharing?

▶ Do I know people who have job shared? Can I talk with them about their experiences?

Telecommuting

You don't have to go to work if the work can come to you. Instead of commuting long distances or moving to find work, you can telecommute almost anywhere in the world via phone, fax, and modem. There are already more than 9 million "lone eagles" in the United States, with more than five hundred corporations offering work-at-home job options.[6] The U.S. Department of Transportation predicts that telecommuters will account for nearly 15 percent of the workforce by 2002.[7]

This move toward telecommuting is fueled by several global trends. Manufacturing, which requires workers on site, is declining, while information services are a growing force in national and world economies. Information can be easily accessed, processed, and distributed electronically anywhere—including your home—through increasingly affordable and powerful computers connected via telephone, satellite, and the Internet.

The flattening of corporate hierarchies, an early result of this information revolution, is accelerating the demand for even more direct, instantaneous communication. Teleconferencing can stand in for some face-to-face meetings, if necessary, but many projects can be conceived, planned, contracted, executed, completed, and paid between participants who never meet. Cellular phones make communication possible from any point on the globe, with no need for an office. When an office is essential, one can be rented anywhere. Airports, hotels, and business parks already offer temporary office cubicles, meeting rooms, and support services for the "migrant workers" of this new age.

Telecommuting is just one facet of an ongoing revolution in the fundamental nature of work. The changes this revolution will bring, including both its benefits and its dangers, are almost impossible to predict—just as no one at the turn of the century knew the enormous impact the internal combustion engine would have on agriculture, city life, the environment, and world history. In the short term, however, we can foresee many obvious benefits.

Companies will spend fewer resources on transportation, parking, child care, food services, middle management, and on building, operating, and maintaining offices. Work will become more flexible and thus more productive. Although a wholesale move in this direction confronts the old "command and control" management philosophy, employers are mostly interested in results.

Telecommuting works for both traditional employment, whether full- or part-time, and for self-employment or freelancing. Telecommuters can work for one or many employers from a home in the suburbs or a cabin in the mountains. In many professions, office apparel will become a curiosity. The complete or partial elimination of the daily commute will save time, lower stress, and conserve fossil fuel and the parent will be there when the kids come home from school. What's more, studies show that people feel they are up to 20 percent more productive when they work at home.

Why Telecommute?

You may find several good reasons to consider telecommuting as your preferred work environment:

Eliminating your commute.   No matter how you cut it, working out of a home office saves time. Even if your commute is as short as 30 minutes a day each way, you can save 240 hours (10 days) a year.

Saving money.   You slash your clothing, food, and commuting costs. Lunch is out of your refrigerator, and your commute may be the five seconds it takes you to walk from your bedroom to your den office.

Achieving balance.   You have more time for your family's needs. You can manage illnesses, school, homework, sports events, special projects, and lunches.

Keeping your roots.   By going online, you can take advantage of business opportunities, even complex projects, wherever they arise, without having to pull up stakes and move your home and family.

Building your own business.   You can get a preview of what it would be like to be out on your own. You can create your own working space, manage your time creatively, and moonlight more easily if you want to. You can build up a small base of clients while working on your full-time job. You can also get a sense—before cutting the umbilical cord—of whether or not you are an entrepreneur.

Ask yourself the following questions:

▶ What advantages or disadvantages are there in being a telecommuter?

▶ Would telecommuting be feasible in my current job? Could I negotiate a telecommuting arrangement?

▶ Do I know others who are already telecommuting in my organization or elsewhere?

▶ Do my work skills lend themselves to telecommuting?

Starting Your Own Business

With the security of permanent jobs fading, many people are moving out of organizations and capitalizing on their skills and the needs of the marketplace. The jobs are out there, but in smaller organizations. Large companies contract out work that was formerly done in-house, and niche companies are springing up to fill the gap. Two-thirds of all the new jobs in America are in organizations of twenty or fewer employees.

Technology has leveled the playing field between large and small businesses. You can set up a fully functional office for less than $3,000, then use the Internet to show your target audience your products or services or to find information, contacts, advice, or mentors. Your advantage as a former employee is that you know better than most what your former employer needs. This puts you in a great position to fill that need with your own niche company—a business whose horizons you can then proceed to expand.

Many of the experts on start-ups advise you to stay small and work lean until you are well established. You can expect to work long hours and pinch pennies for a few years—but successful entrepreneurs have to be willing to endure hardship and hard work to build their own businesses. A recent tongue-in-cheek quiz in *Inc.* magazine tested the potential bootstrapper's willingness to do whatever it takes.[8] Questions included such indicators as these:

► Are you willing to work eighty or more hours a week?

► Would you visit your family at mealtimes or crash wedding receptions to ensure basic nutrition?

► Would you be willing to start up your office in an abandoned broom closet?

► Would you accumulate fifty credit cards and charge them all up to the line?

If you can answer yes to all the above, you may be ready to go out on your own and start a new business. But, that's not all it takes to succeed.

Many businesses that are now household words were started on a shoestring:

► Tom Monaghan bought a bankrupt pizzeria for $900. Domino's current sales are at $1 billion.

► Eighteen-year-old Joyce C. Hall began selling picture postcards by mail order in 1910. Within months, Hall had cleared $200. He added greeting cards in 1912. Current Hallmark sales are $3.1 billion.

► Brothers Ernest and Julio Gallo started making wine in 1933 in a rented warehouse in Modesto, California. They bought equipment on ninety-day term and sold their first six thousand gallons to a Chicago wine distributor. Current sales are $580 million.

Recent information reveals that the most successful start-ups tend to be

► headed by people with ten or more years of experience in the same industry or profession

> ▶ in high-tech and small manufacturing industries

> ▶ founded by people who have started other successful businesses

> ▶ team efforts by two or more partners

A growing number of entrepreneuring courses in colleges and universities, however, coupled with a common desire to be self-sufficient rather than dependent on large organizations, seem to be propelling younger first-timers into successful business start-ups. Jerry Yang and David Filo, the inventors of Yahoo, the popular Internet directory, turned a hobby into a product and became multimillionaires. Cisco Systems was founded by a young husband-and-wife team and is now worth $31 billion. Kinko's, founded by USC student Paul Oralea, has brought a "new way to office" to more than eight hundred locations. If you can meet an unfilled need or expand an existing service in a new way, experience is not an absolute requirement.[9]

Why Start Your Own Business?

You want to test an idea for a product or service that you know will make it.   Sometimes you just know you've got an idea whose time has come and you can't stop until you test it out. You've tested the idea with several people you respect, and they agree that it will sell.

Your current organization won't support product development for your idea.   You know suppliers or customers who would purchase your product or service in an instant, but you've been unable to persuade your current organization of its merits.

You are convinced it's the only way to achieve the income you want.   You've worked hard for many years but feel you are underpaid. You are a master in a profession or trade that is in demand. You know people who respect and depend on your work and who will hire you as an independent business owner.

You do your best work when you run your own show. You require independence and autonomy and like calling the shots. You dislike being supervised by people who can't match your skill, experience, and business sense.

Ask yourself the following questions:

▶ Am I experienced in the area in which I want to start a business?

▶ Can I take a risk and have the patience to put up with hard times for a while?

▶ Have I done my research on the need for the product or service?

▶ Are there colleagues who will work the business with me?

What Have You Learned?

As you can see, there are many ways to package your work life—perhaps many more than you suspected. Assess your options. Which arrangement best suits the kinds of work that are available in your field? Which match the sort of environment you would like to work in? Which best fit the way you would like to live your personal life?

Now you are aware of the many elements that can go into strong employability and a sense of running your own career. Keep these packaging options in mind as you read the next two chapters. They will help you put all the pieces of the Web of Work together in ways that may surprise you.

Building Your Capability Portfolio

*T*HESE FINAL TWO CHAPTERS tie it all together! You will see how to combine your purpose, passion, profession, and capability with the needs of others—and, in the process, put together a stable work scenario for yourself. You will create your very own Capability Portfolio™.

My goal is to show you how to leverage economic, technological, societal, industrial, and organizational trends, as well as the human needs they address to create new services and products. These trends, changes, and needs are the source of new work for you and others. Every problem, every business issue, every industry or organization trend is loaded with new possibilities, new services, and new products; people who see them coming can turn them into powerful new work opportunities.

The Web of Work Continually Evolves

We know that two contemporary trends—companies cutting support staff to concentrate on core functions, and people working longer and harder with fewer resources—have created all kinds of new work opportunities:

▶ Automated teller machines

▶ Building custodial services

▶ Gardening services

▶ Graphic design services

▶ Home cleaning services

▶ Household workers

▶ Overnight delivery services

▶ Personal shoppers

▶ Photocopying services

▶ Process engineering services

▶ Publication services

▶ Take-out restaurants

▶ Tax planning services

▶ Word-processing services

These trends not only generate new jobs, they also cause many of the layoffs in the old organizations. This is part of the natural evolution of work caused by advances in technology, world economic evolution, and new ways of addressing human needs. The net result, however, is more jobs. As you can see, not only are companies' support functions still addressed—by small companies taking advantage of niche opportunities—but the changes in employees' work environments and lifestyles also create new job opportunities. People who see these trends evolving will anticipate the changes in how human needs must be addressed. They will create thousands of new products and services that will be in wide demand to meet those needs.

In this chapter, you will see how to take a basic human need, trend, or issue and shape it into a new work niche for yourself. *Trend catching is a crucial mindset; proposal making is its entrepreneurial sidekick.* Together, these two capabilities will help you anticipate needs and create work where others only complain or become fearful or obsolete. I want to help you develop such a capability mindset not because I think that everyone ought to start a small business; rather, I'm convinced that, by perceiving and thinking this way, you will respond better to the challenges of tomorrow's world of work, no matter what organization you're in.

One Idea Can Change the Work of Many

Every business that you can name came into being at the moment someone saw a basic need that wasn't being fulfilled and figured out a way to fulfill it. To show you how the need for the business arises, we can illustrate with an example that has affected all our lives profoundly.

1. A new problem arises, or an old problem becomes apparent to more and more people. (While the steam engine brings rapid mass transportation over long distances, personal and local transportation is limited by the speed of the horse, the expense of stabling and caring for the animals, and the necessity for street cleaning.)

2. A solution is proposed. (A new technology, the internal combustion engine, provides a compact, lightweight, efficient way to power personal vehicles.)

3. Niche companies are formed to meet the changing human need to move small numbers of people and products more quickly, at any time, from

anywhere to anywhere else. (Scores of automobile manufacturers and sales outlets arise to fill different parts of the growing niche: town cars, touring cars, sports cars, trucks, inter-city buses.)

4. Fulfilling the changing needs created by the original niche causes a chain reaction: new niches and new work opportunities, which may grow exponentially. (Petroleum exploration and drilling, refining, gasoline service stations, aviation, automobile parts, highway cafes, tourist courts, campgrounds, motels, airlines, towing services, collision insurance, auto detailing.)

The automobile is an example of a niche that grew to become a critical aspect of our national economy. Most niches, however, tend to be small or short-lived, quickly superseded by technological developments or other changes. One automobile industry niche that appeared and disappeared early was the electric car, but this niche has reappeared nearly a century later because of changes in society's attitude toward the environment. Another short-lived niche that has probably disappeared forever is gas lighting. Although it brightened city life in the latter part of the last century, the need for it was quickly obviated by the new technology of generating and transmitting electricity—a safer, cheaper, cleaner, and far more versatile service.

Trends for Our Time

But you don't need to be, or perhaps even want to be, an entrepreneur on a grand scale. All you need is a niche large enough for one person—a little larger, if you are ambitious about hiring some people to help you.

To find that niche, start with a trend. The natural chain of events is

1. discover a trend

2. identify a need

3. find a niche

4. create a new product or service

Let's explore this concept by playing a game: "Connect the Trends." Four trends currently affect today's society—trends that we all experience. Take out your pencil and connect each trend on the left with as many new products or services or companies as you can on the right. (If you use a different color for each trend, you'll see more.) This will give you a good sense of how trends generate new or expanded niches.

Connect the Trends

Trend	New Company/Service
Speed as a competitive advantage	**ATMs** **Courier services** **Dating services** **Domino's Pizza**
Working longer hours or extra jobs	**Educational toys** **Fast food** **Fax machines** **FedEx**
Single parent/both parents working	**Finances for Dummies** **Health clubs** **Kinko's** **Maid for You**
Thousands of small business start-ups	**Modems** **Office-on-Call** **Personal shoppers** **Personal trainers** **Pies-on-the-Run** **24-hour grocery stores** **We Network You**

After you've drawn your lines, see if you can list three or four other services, products, niches, or businesses that have developed as a result of each of the trends. This activity is fun to do. It will help you develop the mental muscle and systemic relational thinking that you need to connect significant trends with new niche opportunities—giving you an entrepreneurial advantage few others will have.

Suitcase on Wheels

As another way to develop those mental muscles relating trends and needs to new niches, let's work the exercise in reverse. Let's take one new product and see if we can intuit the problems, needs, trends, and issues that caused someone to develop and market it. This new viewpoint will help you see the Web of Work as an integrated structure and think like an entrepreneur.

Our new product is the suitcase on wheels. In the past decade you've seen more and more of these in air terminals—you may even own one. Sometimes it's a single piece of utilitarian luggage trundling along behind a businessperson; sometimes it's a whole fleet of stylish designer cases being herded toward the baggage counter by a vacationing family. (The original rolling suitcase, I have heard, was invented by a pilot who was just tired of schlepping his luggage.)

Scan the following list of issues and trends. What do you think were the most important in catalyzing the invention of this new product?

▶ Damaged suitcases

▶ People in a hurry

▶ Fear of lost luggage

▶ Reducing stress and backaches

▶ Making plane connections on time

▶ Airlines' greater acceptance of carry-ons

▶ Making transportation easier

▶ Increased business travel

List as many additional trends and needs as you can think of, even those with the flimsiest connections. Then think about these trends and needs. Work forward again: Can you think of any other ways these same or similar needs might be addressed?

Tremors in the Web

Now, let's spend some time charting how a small event in one industry—the idea of a suitcase on wheels—affected a broad range of industries, professions, organizations, and jobs. The more you can see how all the sectors of the Web are interrelated, especially in a time of change, the greater will be your perspective, and your ability to spot opportunities. Perhaps you'll even identify the need for new products and services. This knowledge will help give you a stable platform in an apparently unstable world.

Picture the suitcase on wheels. If you had the idea to make such a thing, what professions would you need to engage to test your idea? Some, of course, would be important early in the design phase; others would be brought in to make it beautiful, to market and sell it, and so forth. For now, think about the most important professions that you would turn to.

Add any professions you think of to those shown on the following list.

▶ Advertising

▶ Chemical engineering

▶ Design engineering

▶ Ergonomics

▶ Marketing

▶ Mechanical engineering

▶ Sales

▶ Sports medicine

Now, what industries would have to be involved in some way to make this idea a reality? You can probably think of several that haven't occurred to me. Add them to the growing Web.

▶ Consumer goods

▶ Health care

▶ Plastics

▶ Manufacturing

▶ Textiles

▶ Transportation

Obviously, the wheeled suitcase idea affected many organizations, some positively and others—those that didn't see the need—negatively. The following list, compiled from our research, shows some of the organizations and classes of organizations that have felt the impact. Some were created, others had to adapt, by delivering new products and using new technology, in order to stay competitive. You may know of others.

▶ Department stores

▶ Discount stores

▶ Samsonite

▶ The Sharper Image

▶ Textile organizations

▶ The makers of Velcro

Finally, thousands of jobs have been affected. Hundreds of new jobs came into being, and others faded. Following are just a few of the jobs that were probably affected by the suitcase on wheels:

▶ Advertising account executive	▶ Graphic designer
▶ Accountant	▶ Inventory controller
▶ Aircraft designer	▶ Market research analyst
▶ Baggage handler	▶ Packer
▶ Cab driver	▶ Plant manager
▶ Color designer	▶ Porter
▶ Customer service representative	▶ Salesperson
▶ Ergonomics engineer	▶ Tele-sales operator
▶ Fabrications specialist	▶ Textile technician
▶ Flight attendant	▶ Truckers

In summary, the trends led to an idea that created waves and aftershocks for thousands of people in many professions, industries, organizations, and jobs on the Web of Work. This is just one of tens of thousands of examples of how the Web continues to grow and evolve every day. The more of the system you can see, the more powerful and stable your career future. The more adept you become at spotting trends, the more secure you will feel and the more creative you will be at running your own career.

In the next chapter, you will discover how you can flesh out the bones of your idea, then either propose new products or services to your current organization or create a new business to exploit the opportunity to fulfill another human need. The end product will be your detailed Capability Portfolio™.

The Capable Entrepreneur

MANY EXPERTS TELL YOU to become an entrepreneur, but few tell you how, or even why, and those who do often focus narrowly on the aspect of raising money and starting your own business. I am more interested in encouraging you to use entrepreneurial methods to discover human needs in a changing society—and to address those needs in ways that let you design your own niche and work environment.

In the process of learning to be a capable entrepreneur, you will learn how to build your own Capability Portfolio™. Capable entrepreneurship requires the intersection of seven different but related actions.

People who master these abilities as entrepreneurs or as employees are not frightened by world-altering trends; instead, they see change as a natural, universal, eternal phenomenon. They sense opportunity; they know they are capable of participating and contributing: "How can I address this need, ride this trend, in ways that are good for me and for the community?"

This chapter will help you practice these thinking skills while building your Capability Portfolio. I have recreated the Capability Portfolio that I use in my seminars in the appendix on page 265. There is a blank space for you to fill out and you can study the completed portion that reflects the example I use in this chapter. As you read this chapter, build your own Capability

C atching the drift of emerging trends and needs in society, technology, and industry

A nticipating new niches, products, or services that meet those needs

P roposing realistic options and solutions

A nalyzing the benefits to organizations, industries, customers, and the bottom line

B olstering your case with prior accomplishments, competencies, and service role expertise

L everaging your reputation in your profession, industry, and organization

E ngaging your services in accord with your desired compensation, preferred employment package, and environmental needs

Portfolio by responding to the ideas presented here. Unlike a résumé, which shows only your past accomplishments, your Capability Portfolio focuses on your present and future. The more you practice this entrepreneurial mindset, the more confident you'll become and the more options for contribution and wealth creation you will see.

Catch the Drift of Emerging Trends and Needs

Innovation happens because society changes: a human need changes or grows. New methods and new activities are discovered or invented. Most of us would rather not deal with change. We like our established ways of living and coping. We grow comfortable with routine. If we had to plan each day anew, we would be constantly unsettled. And yet, we deal comfortably with change in many ways. When our record player wears out, we shop for a CD player and marvel at how much better it sounds. We adapt to fluoridated toothpaste and find ourselves spending less on dental work. We don't experience most trends as sudden windstorms—rather, as gentle breezes that we become aware of gradually.

The trick to thinking like an entrepreneur is seeing change coming and adapting your thinking earlier than most. If you were among the first to understand that CDs would entirely supplant records, you could probably have foreseen at least a few consequences of that impending change and thought up new products and services before anyone else: CD carriers, automobile CD players, and used CD stores.

Think about recent changes in places and items you see every day:

▶ Art

▶ Music

▶ Web sites

▶ Television

▶ Bookstores

▶ Supermarkets

▶ Your neighborhood

Both content and context are important. When thinking about bookstores, for example, consider not only current titles and topics on the shelves but also the number, sizes, and kinds of bookstores that are sprouting up or fading from the scene. Raise your trend sensitivity by talking with others about the changes they observe.

No one can watch all the trends going on in this fast-changing world. Your best bet is to focus on certain contexts or settings. The major classes of trends to watch are societal (the aging of America, the growing gap between rich and poor), political (the spread of democracy, the rise of religious fundamentalism), and technological (computerization, Internet, telecommuting). To stay alert to new work possibilities, pay particular attention to trends in your profession, industry or organization. Trends are sometimes easiest to detect at the industry level.

Futurists like Faith Popcorn make careers out of trend watching. Popcorn's 1996 book, *Clicking: 16 Trends to Future Fit Your Life, Your Work, and Your Business,* is an easy-to-read distillation of trends that she says will shake up every industry. Scan Popcorn's top ten. Which trends will have a major impact on your industry, your organization, or your job? How many new

Popcorn's Top Trends

Cocooning—*staying at home*

Fantasy Adventure—*risk-free escapes*

Small Indulgences—*affordable luxuries*

Egonomics—*personal statement*

99 Lives—*busy lifestyle*

Cashing Out—*choosing a simpler way of living*

Being Alive—*searching for wellness*

Down-Aging—*recapturing our childhood*

Vigilante Consumer—*marketplace political tactics*

S.O.S. (Save Our Society)—*protecting the planet*

Trend: Stick with the Core Competencies

Benefits to company:	*Increase revenue by outsourcing*
	Stay focused on primary strategies
	Reduce overhead
	Reduce regulations-compliance burden
New niches:	*Payroll companies*
	Tax-compliance consultants and companies
	Employee-benefits companies
	Claims administration consultants and companies
	Outsourcing brokers

products, services, and companies can you think of that address the trends in your industry? Do you see any unfulfilled needs? Make a list of all the ways your organization or profession might address some of these needs. Write down even remote possibilities in the "Catch the Trends" section of the Capability Portfolio.

Hold on to these ideas. You'll use them at the second step, when you start anticipating niches.

Trends in Your Profession, Industry, and Organization

Changes in society, technology, and other contexts create new needs to be fulfilled, and new opportunities for those who are alert to the trends. As I pointed out earlier, farming out noncore competencies not only has allowed companies to downsize and work more efficiently, it also has given entrepreneurs the opportunity to create many new companies whose sole purpose is to provide financial and other services to them. These new companies, highly focused on the new corporate need to obtain outside financial services, hire specialists to fill new jobs. In the long run, everybody benefits.

In my consultations with clients over the last ten years, I have focused mainly on trends in professions, industries, and organizations. To be ahead of the curve, to be acting with rather than catching up to trends, you must establish practices, conduct conversations, even put together support networks to help you scan these three domains.

List the names of three people you respect when it comes to each domain. Tell each person that you are building your capability as an entrepreneur and would like his or her help in seeing new work possibilities. Ask for a one-hour interview and offer to share the results of your investigation. Start with three basic questions:

1. Name three trends that you believe will cause important changes in your (profession, industry, organization) over the next three to five years.

2. For each trend, discuss who will be affected and how.

3. What new products or services could address those trends?

Listen especially for trends, patterns, and themes that are cited more than once—the more it recurs, the stronger the trend. Then concentrate on trends that engage your passion and purpose, require your professional mastery, and satisfy the human needs you care most about. Doing so will help make this more than an intellectual exercise—you'll be discovering something about yourself and maybe even seeing a new business opportunity.

Anticipate New Niches

In the suitcase-on-wheels example, trends in stress management, business speed, time consciousness, and increased travel made someone think of a way to adapt an ordinary suitcase to satisfy changing needs. How did the inventor experience these trends? What made a suitcase with wheels flash in this person's mind? This is the kind of thinking I want you to learn and practice. It's also the next step in building your Capability Portfolio.

Examples of niche makers abound in all the new businesses and products around us:

▶ **Problem:** It's hard to navigate through the Internet.
Solution: *Netscape*

▶ **Problem:** People don't have time to cook healthful, low-cal meals.
Solution: *Diets-to-Go—*
prepared meals consisting of 1,200-1,500-1,800 calories and other nutritional requirements—you can pick them up twice weekly or they'll deliver them to your home for an extra fee

▶ **Problem:** Someone burned her hands on a hot steering wheel.
Solution: *Auto Cool Window Blockers—the cardboard protectors for your car window*

Review your interviews. Scan the trends you jotted down on your Capability Portfolio. Then do a little brainstorming:

▶ Which trends grab you?

▶ What new needs do these trends create?

▶ What new products or services would satisfy these needs?

Think up ten ways you could address each of the major trends with a new product or service. If you get stuck, ask the person nearest you—at home, on a plane, in your office. We've shown a real-life, nonfanciful example in the box "Anticipating Niches."

Finally, review your key trends and the products or services that you might create to meet each trend. Choose a product or service that you want

ANTICIPATING NICHES	
Trend	**Service/Product**
99 Lives	*Electronic bill paying*
	Mail order catalog
	Errand service
	Gift purchasing service
	In-home cook
	Personal trainer
	TV shopping network
	Web site designer
	Diets-to-Go

to explore more fully, note them in your Capability Portfolio, and proceed to the next step.

Propose Options

Many people see opportunities, but few take the time to craft an offer that can't be refused. If you see a need and a solution and have a picture of what it would take and what the result would look like, you can make it happen or enlist experts to get the ball rolling.

As you construct your proposal for a new product or service and how you expect to deliver it, you must address three issues, listed below. I have been particularly impressed with an entrepreneurial venture in my community, Diets-to-Go. This business prepares meals to your specifications and delivers them to your home. Last year when I was trying to lose weight, I ordered 1,500-calorie, low-fat, low-sodium meals. They were prepared and delivered to my home once a week. The company made money, and I ate nutritious meals and lost fifteen pounds! Note how Diets-to-Go met each of the issues listed below. As you continue, fill out your Capability Portfolio.

1. *Clarify the need you are addressing.* Focus on one niche. Choose a product or service that you are well-positioned to offer or that addresses an important need in your industry or organization.

Diets-to-Go: *Prepares three meals a day to assist busy clients in their efforts to lose weight.*

2. Identify your target market.   Exactly who needs what you propose and is in a position to endorse the offer? If it's a proposal to a person in an organization, does she have the money or the authority to make it happen? Can she follow through on it? Show her how your offer meets her major interests and concerns.

Diets-to-Go: *Middle-class men and women in Fairfax County, Virginia who want to lose weight but don't have the time or discipline to prepare appropriate meals.*

3. Make the offer.   Craft the offer in one sentence. Describe the product or service that you are offering in a way that engages the recipient's passion, sounds believable, and demonstrates that you can fill a need in ways that no one else can.

Diets-to-Go: *"You tell us how many calories and any other dietary specifications and we'll prepare three meals a day for you. You can pick them up or pay for delivery."*

As you record your work in your Capability Portfolio, remember that each step takes thinking and rehearsal. Phrase the offer clearly, succinctly, and in a way that addresses the recipient's basic needs. Find out what will move others to accept your proposal; include it in the initial offer. Create a detailed word picture of what will happen if your proposal becomes a reality. Know in advance who your recipient or recipients will be. Should you craft your presentation for someone you haven't met? For more than one person? Find out what they do, how they think, and how your proposal might address their interests.[1] Finally, rehearse the offer by role play—not the whole discussion, just the initial proposal. Get feedback. Make your presentation paint the picture of this product or service so clearly in the minds of the recipients that they can't refuse your offer.

Analyze the Benefits

It goes without saying you have to *build* your case before you can make your case. This means research. Find out all you can about the company or target groups to whom you are making the offer. Use your analytical skill to get at the significant facts. Do at least a threefold analysis of the benefits: to the company, to customers, and to the industry. Note your findings in your Capability Portfolio.

1. Benefits to the company.   How will your product or service address the company's needs? What will happen that isn't happening now? How will it affect work, productivity, and the company's reputation? Will it save money? Will it use time more efficiently? What are the short-term and long-term financial benefits of your offer?

2. Benefits to customer.   List as many benefits as you can for customers or individuals. Think in terms of time, resources, money, reputation, results, and so on. Come up with as many benefits as you can. Then talk to some people who know the customer or individuals and adapt your list.

3. Benefits to the industry.   In the case of creating a new product or service, you might be affecting other companies or organizations in the industry. Will this have widespread impact? Where? How?

Bolster Your Case

Will the recipient of your offer believe you can deliver what you promise? Your track record is crucial. What have you accomplished that demonstrates your credibility? Have you delivered similar products or services before? to whom? with what result? If you've already performed this service for fifty satisfied people, you have a track record and a list of satisfied people who will vouch for your ability. Take stock of the competencies you must have in order to deliver the product or service. Suppose, for example, that you are offering a new kind of musical service:

Proposed service: Provide customized music tapes for each member of a family or other individuals or groups.

Prior Accomplishments:

1. Worked at Tower Records for two years; listened to about one hundred tapes a week

2. Guitarist and pianist for sixteen years

3. Sound engineer at high-school plays for two years

Competencies:

✓ Recording music on tape
✓ Interviewing musicians and others
✓ Writing instructions for taping and ad copy
✓ Time management
✓ Music knowledge

Think about the capabilities you will need most in order to make your offer a reality. What are your technical and managerial competencies? Which service roles will best enable you to provide the product or service? What positions do you excel in—resource provider, strategist, project manager, or specialist? How can you demonstrate your abilities?

In the space provided in your Capability Portfolio™:

1. List three accomplishments that demonstrate your ability to make your proposed product or service a reality. Be specific and detailed. Use accomplishments that speak powerfully to your recipients. Use their language to tell your story.

2. List at least six competencies that support your ability to achieve the concept you are proposing.

3. List the service role or roles that bolster your case (from pages 215–218).

This is the step where you put meat on the bones. What will it take to provide the product or service? Show clearly why *you* are the person most capable of making it happen. Demonstrate your capability so dramatically that people can't refuse you.

Leverage Your Reputation and Network

People who know your work and have been pleased with your contribution to them or their organization are the best public relations source you have. Survey your network for people who will vouch for your ability to deliver on your concept—current and former colleagues, managers, customers, and vendors. Include everyone whose professional respect you've earned.

What is your reputation in the industry, your organization, and your profession? The more powerful your reputation, the more power you have to negotiate what you want and to build a stable work life. If you can get the support of one or two key people, your position is even stronger. Who is willing to put his name on the line for you? to support or sponsor you? Whose names can you mention? List these people in the space provided in your Capability Portfolio™.

If you're moving into new territory—becoming entrepreneurial in a new setting or for the first time—scan your support network even more broadly. People remember those who deliver well on promises, on time. Search your community, school, religious, or political endeavors for people who know what you can do. Share your proposal with them and ask whether they would be willing to recommend you. You may be surprised at your reservoir of support!

Engage Your Services

Even before your proposal is accepted, think about what you expect to get in return. What sort of environment do you wish to work in? How much do you expect to be paid for your services? Whether you're working for yourself or for the organization to which you're offering the proposal, you should always know what your ideas and contributions are worth as well has how you want to work, both now and in the future.

While I was working on my Ph.D., a major airline hired me to redesign the curriculum and approach of their flight attendant training. My dissertation research involved finding reliable behavioral indicators of what was required for powerful customer service. I came up with nine indicators that became the basis of recruiting, selection, and training. I loved the work, and I knew that we had accomplished a great deal in the first year.

I wanted to keep working there to implement the results of the study. After the first year, I knew they needed me more than I needed them. I went to the human resources vice president and negotiated my contract. Much to his chagrin (an hour of pacing around, smoking, and telling me that my request was impossible), he ended up giving me just what I asked for— half-time work at twice the salary, an office in the headquarters building, and secretarial support. That day I learned the value of knowing my own capabilities. Negotiations have never been quite the same.

When negotiating your contract, pay special attention to the following three elements of your working conditions:

▶ Employment factors

▶ Environmental factors

▶ Compensation options

Be clear about what you want in each of these areas. Know your priorities: you can negotiate more effectively by offering concessions in areas that are less important to you. Which of the following matter most to you and which least? Review the matrix on page 219 for your favored employment and environment factors.

1. *Employment factors:*

Full-time
Part-time
Contract
Temp
Telecommute

2. *Environmental factors:*

Working hours
Location
Commute
Team
Other

3. *Compensation options:*

Paid by the job
Paid by the hour

Commission

Royalty

Percentage of profits

Patent or trademark

Barter

Other

In the space provided in the Capability Portfolio, list your preferred employment, environment, and compensation options.

If you are making your proposal to your employer, review your compensation options—with help from your support network, if possible. Do you want a percentage of the profits? a salary that grows with profitability and customer satisfaction? patent rights? an option to start your own business? You might even prefer not to change a thing. Put your proposal in writing. Be clear, support your arguments, and have in mind a fallback position. Be open to developing other options as you talk with your advisers.

These are the seven steps necessary for developing your own Capability Portfolio. The more you practice them, the more entrepreneurial you'll become. You'll see opportunities others miss. You'll surprise customers with your service. You'll be improving other peoples' lives while increasing your own capabilities.

As you practice the seven steps to building a Capability Portfolio, you will be mastering the Web of Work. You will be building stable work in unstable times. You will be running your career. Good luck!

APPENDIX

Capability Portfolio

Catch the Trends	**A**nticipate New Niches	**P**ropose Options	**A**nalyze the Benefits
• Overweight people	• Prepare meals for people • Diet books • Exercise shows	1. *Clarify your option:* Develop meals with specific calories, fat, and other specifications	1. *Customers:* Eat right, lose weight, save time
• Little time to grocery shop	• Health clubs • Aerobic classes • Dietary shopping services	2. *Choose the recipient:* Middle-class, overweight working people in Virginia suburbs	2. *Company & Reputation:* Low overhead Expand through referrals
• Lack of nutrition knowledge	• • •	3. *Craft the offer:* "Tell us your dietary requirements and we will pre-package meals for pick-up or delivery."	3. *Bottom Line:* Affordable, Targeted Profitable 4. *Industry:* New niche, applicable for healthy and sick people

Catch the Trends	**A**nticipate New Niches	**P**ropose Options	**A**nalyze the Benefits
• _____	• • •	1. *Clarify your option:*	1. *Customers:*
• _____	• • •	2. *Choose the recipient:*	2. *Company & Reputation:*
• _____	• • •	3. *Craft the offer:*	3. *Bottom Line:* 4. *Industry:*

Bolster **Your Case**   **L**everage Your **Reputation**   **E**ngage Your **Services**

---

1. *Accomplishment:*
   Ran school kitchen
   w/ unique meals

2. *Accomplishment:*
   Nutrition coach for
   individuals with 50%
   weight loss

3. *Accomplishment:*
   Hospital dietician
   for three years

Competencies:
   ✓ Nutrition knowledge
   ✓ Food preparation
   ✓ Food packaging
   ✓ Marketing
   ✓ Organizing
   ✓ Meal preparation

1. *Organization:*
   Founders

2. *Profession:*
   Known in hospital,
   school communities

3. *Industry:*
   Active in Weight
   Watchers, nutritional
   counseling

4. *Community:*
   PTA social director,
   Health club
   fitness coach

1. *Employment factors:*
   Full-time
   Part-time
   Temporary

2. *Environmental factors:*
   No travel
   Flexible hours
   Passion for cooking
   Promotes health

3. *Compensation:*
   Weekly fee
   Percentage of profits
   Potential for
   franchising

Service Role(s):
   ☑ *Specialist*   ☐ *Resource Provider*
   ☑ *Project Manager*   ☐ *Strategist*

---

1. *Accomplishment:*

2. *Accomplishment:*

3. *Accomplishment:*

Competencies:
   ✓
   ✓
   ✓
   ✓
   ✓
   ✓

1. *Organization:*

2. *Profession:*

3. *Industry:*

4. *Community:*

1. *Employment factors:*

2. *Environmental factors:*

3. *Compensation:*

Service Role(s):
   ☐ *Specialist*   ☐ *Resource Provider*
   ☐ *Project Manager*   ☐ *Strategist*

Notes

Chapter 2: Addressing Your Needs

1. You may define some of these needs a bit differently. That's fine. The purpose of distinguishing and defining them is to help create a common map. The words don't matter as much as the general ideas—the needs—they denote.

2. Most adult development theorists claim that addressing each of the twelve needs is also the primary focus and function of adults. Some of the needs are especially pervasive in our lives. In my Lifescapes™ workshop for people "in transition," people assess the status of their lives in each of the twelve areas and formulate life plans that help them achieve their goals in different areas.

    In our WorkPower™ Career Workshops, using an instrument called The Twenty-Year Journey™, participants look back ten years, examine the present, and project ten years into the future regarding their goals and aspirations in each of the twelve areas. Many people say this meditative exercise is the most important part of the workshop. They see that work/career is only one of twelve important adult needs and that they must balance their focus and energy to take care of the others.

3. The unfortunate truth about many of our large, multilevel organizations is that some peoples' jobs are far removed from the human needs they are there to serve. In hospitals, until very recently, admitting receptionists in emergency rooms appeared more concerned with insurance forms and other administrivia than in taking care of the patient. Today, most emergency rooms are organized in teams, each designated as the caretaker for an individual patient. Without this sense of close connection, people get lost in the system. They end up just doing jobs, such as processing forms, rather than taking care of people. Consequently, they also lose a sense of contribution and meaning in their daily work.

Chapter 4: Learn to Live Your Passion

1. Deal Me In™ is a trademark of Career Systems, Inc., distributed by MasteryWorks™.

2. Barnhart, *Five Rituals of Wealth*, 58–59.

Chapter 7: Mastery: Your Big Career Advantage

1. Schön, *Educating the Reflective Practitioner*, 16.

2. Farren, "Specialist or Generalist."

3. Hartwick and Farren, "Specialists or Generalists," 123.

4. Dr. Bloom's study is detailed in a gem of a book by Donald Clifton and Paula Nelson, *Soar with Your Strengths*. Dr. Bloom's study, the Development of Talent Project, analyzed the careers of world-class concert pianists, sculptors, research mathematicians, research neurologists, Olympic swimmers, and tennis champions.

Chapter 12: Is Your Organization Viable?

1. Brokaw, "Truth about Start-Ups."

2. L. D. DeSimone, chairman and CEO of 3M, quoted in Perspectives, "How Can Big Companies Keep the Entrepreneurial Spirit Alive?" 184.

3. Ibid., 190–192, quoting Charles P. Holt, vice president of the Wilson Center for Research and Technology at Xerox Corporation in Rochester, New York.

4. Stewart, "Planning a Career."

5. Stewart, "Get with the New Power Game."

6. Ibid.

7. Stewart, "Planning a Career."

8. Caggiano, "Do You Have What It Takes?"

9. Employee Ownership Report, January/February 1995, "Case Study: Physicians Sales and Service."

10. Fierman, "Winning Ideas from Maverick Managers."

11. Tully, "You'll Never Guess Who Really Makes . . ."

12. Helgesen, *Web of Inclusion*.

Chapter 13: Jobs

1. William Bridges coined the phrase "the dejobbing of America" in his excellent book *Job Shift: How to Prosper in a Workplace without Jobs*. The best treatment to date on the decline of the job as the basis for lifetime work, *Job Shift* shows why searching for jobs will not be nearly as important a skill in the future as looking at needs and shaping your work to deliver needed products or services.

Chapter 14: Technology, Reengineering, and Customers

1. The Economist, "Kindergarten That Will Change the World."

2. Valencia, ed., *At Work,* 4.

3. Ibid., 19.

Chapter 16: Creating Your Work Niche

1. The ideas and exercises in chapters 16 through 18 have been built into a MasteryWorks™ workshop called "Building Your Capability Portfolio™—Working on Your Terms."

2. The four roles and self-assessment instrument were adapted from Thomas Stewart, "Building Careers in a World without Managers."

3. Ibid.

Chapter 17: Working on Your Own Terms

1. Henkoff, "Winning the New Career Game."

2. Ibid.

3. Halal, "Rise of the Knowledge Worker."

4. The National Association of Temporary and Staffing Services serves a broad cross section of firms placing temporary workers at all levels in all industries.

5. Halal, "Rise of the Knowledge Worker."

6. Warner, "Working at Home."

7. Cox, *Redefining Corporate Soul.*

8. Caggiano, "Do You Have What it Takes?"

9. One of the best-kept secrets in America is the importance of female entrepreneurs in the U.S. economy. Women start roughly 1.75 million new businesses a year. Assuming an average of five hires per company, woman-owned businesses create nearly 9 million new jobs a year. Over a five-year period, 20 million women get jobs with entrepreneurial companies and, according to historical data, 25 percent of these will catch the same bug and start businesses of their own. The primary assets of woman-owned businesses are information, networks, insight, and trained people who will follow the owners to the end of the earth (Silver, *Quantum Companies*). In 1994, 7 million women had sole proprietorships, not including women who owned corporations or partnerships.

Chapter 19: The Capable Entrepreneur

1. Read Getting *to Yes,* by Roger Fisher and William Ury, if you need more insight as to how to get at people's basic interests.

Bibliography

Abarbanel, Karin. *How to Succeed on Your Own: Overcoming the Emotional Roadblocks on the Way from Corporation to Cottage, from Employee to Entrepreneur.* Richmond Hill, Ont., Canada: Fitzhenry & Whiteside, 1994.

Arden, Lynie. *Work At Home.* Boulder: Live Oak, 1996.

Armstrong, Thomas. *7 Kinds of Smart: Identifying and Developing Your Many Intelligences.* London: Penguin Books, 1993.

Baber, Anne, and Lynne Waymon. *How to Fireproof Your Career: Survival Strategies for Volatile Times.* New York: Berkley Books, 1995.

Barker, Joel. *Future Edge: Discovering the New Paradigms of Success.* New York: William Morrow & Co., 1992.

Barnhart, Tod. *The Five Rituals of Wealth: Proven Strategies for Turning the Little You Have into More Than Enough.* New York: Harper Business, 1995.

Bateson, Mary Catherine. *Composing a Life.* New York: Penguin Books, 1990.

Bolles, Richard N. *The 1996 What Color Is Your Parachute? A Practical Manual for Job-Hunters and Career-Changers.* Berkeley: Ten Speed Press, 1996.

Bridges, William. *Job Shifts: How to Prosper in a Workplace without Jobs.* Canada: William Bridges, 1994.

Brokaw, Leslie. "The Truth about Start-Ups." *Inc.,* March 1993: 56–64.

Burkan, Wayne. *Wide Angle Vision: Beat Your Competition by Focusing on Fringe Competitors, Lost Customers, and Rogue Employees.* New York: John Wiley & Sons, 1996.

Caggiano, Christopher. "Do You Have What It Takes?" *Inc.,* August 1995.

Caminiti, Susan. "What Happens to Laid-Off Managers?" *Fortune,* June 13, 1994: 68–78.

Case, John. *Open-Book Management: The Coming Business Revolution.* New York: HarperCollins, 1995.

Charland, William A., Jr. *Career Shifting: Starting Over in a Changing Economy.* Holbrook, Mass.: Bob Adams, 1993.

Chopra, Deepak. *The Seven Spiritual Laws of Success: A Practical Guide to the Fulfillment of Your Dreams.* Novato, Calif.: Amber-Allen & New World Library, 1994.

Clifton, Donald O., and Paula Nelson. *Soar with Your Strengths.* New York: Dell, 1992.

Collins, James C., and Jerry I. Porras. *Built to Last: Successful Habits of Visionary Companies.* New York: HarperCollins, 1994.

Cox, Allan, with Julie Liesse. *Redefining Corporate Soul: Linking Purpose and People.* Burr Ridge, Ill.: Irwin, 1996.

Davis, Stan, and Bill Davidson. *2020 Vision: Transform Your Business Today to Succeed in Tomorrow's Economy.* New York: Fireside, 1991.

Dent, Harry S. *The Great Jobs Ahead: Your Comprehensive Guide to Surviving and Prospering in the Coming Work Revolution.* New York: St. Martins, 1995.

Dibbell, Julian. "Nielsen Rates the Net." *Time,* November 13, 1995: 121.

Ditzler, Jinny S. *Your Best Year Yet!* San Francisco: HarperCollins, 1994.

The Economist. "The Kindergarten That Will Change the World." *The Economist,* March 4, 1995: 63–64.

Employee Ownership Report, January/February 1995. "Case Study: Physicians Sales and Services, Benchmark: Employee Participation." *Inc.,* January 1995.

Falkenstein, Lynda. *Nichecraft: Using Your Specialness to Focus Your Business, Corner Your Market, and Make Customers Seek You Out.* New York: HarperBusiness, 1996.

Farren, Caela. "Specialist or Generalist: Which Are You?" Presentation at the annual meeting of the American Society for Training and Development, Dallas, June 1995.

Fierman, J. "Winning Ideas from Maverick Managers." *Fortune,* February 6, 1995: 66–80.

Fisher, Roger, and David Ury. *Getting to Yes.* New York: Penguin Books, 1991.

Fox, Matthew. *The Reinvention of Work: A New Vision of Livelihood for Our Time.* New York: HarperCollins, 1994.

Frankel, Lois P. *Overcoming Your Strengths: 8 Reasons Why Successful People Derail and How to Get Back on Track.* New York: Harmony Books, 1997.

Gardner, Howard. *Frames of Mind: The Theory of Multiple Intelligences.* New York: HarperCollins, 1993.

Hadley, Joyce. *Part-Time Careers.* Hawthorne, N.J.: Career Press, 1993.

Hakim, Cliff. *We Are All Self-Employed: The New Social Contract for Working in a Changed World.* San Francisco: Berrett-Koehler, 1994.

Halal, William E. "The Rise of the Knowledge Entrepreneur." *The Futurist,* November/December 1996.

Hamel, Gary, and C.K. Prahalad. *Competing for the Future.* Boston: Harvard Business School Press, 1994.

Hammer, Michael, and James Champy. *Reengineering the Corporation: A Manifesto for Business Revolution.* New York: HarperBusiness, 1993.

Handy, Charles. *The Age of Unreason.* Boston: Harvard Business School Press, 1990.

————. *Beyond Certainty: The Changing World of Organizations.* Boston: Harvard Business School Press, 1996.

Hartwick, Peter J., and Caela Farren. "Specialists or Generalists A False Dichotomy: An Important Distinction." In *Future Vision: Ideas, Insights, and Strategies,* edited by Howard Didsbury. Bethesda, Md.: World Future Society, 1996.

Havill, Adrian. *Man of Steel: The Career and Courage of Christopher Reeve.* New York: Signet, 1996.

Helgesen, Sally. *The Web of Inclusion: A New Architecture for Building Great Organizations.* New York: Currency/Doubleday, 1995.

Henkoff, Ronald. "Winning the New Career Game." *Fortune,* May 16, 1994: 40–54.

Hoover's. *Top 2,500 Employers.* Austin, Texas: Hoover's Business Press, 1996.

James, Jennifer. *Thinking in the Future Tense: Leadership Skills for a New Age.* New York: Simon & Schuster, 1996.

Jones, Laurie B. *The Path: Creating Your Mission Statement for Work and for Life.* New York: Hyperion, 1996.

Kennedy Publications. *The Directory of Executive Temporary Placement Firms.* Fitzwilliam, N. H.: Kennedy & Kennedy, 1995.

Koonce, Richard. *Career Power! 12 Winning Habits to Get You from Where You Are to Where You Want to Be.* New York: Amacom, 1994.

Labich, Kenneth. "Why Companies Fail." *Fortune,* November 14, 1994: 52–68.

Larson, Jackie, and Cheri Comstock. *The New Rules of the Job Search Game: Why Today's Managers Hire . . . and Why They Don't.* Holbrook, Mass.: Bob Adams, 1994.

Leonard, George. *Mastery: The Keys to Success and Long-Term Fulfillment.* New York: Plume, 1991.

Levering, Robert, and Milton Moskowitz. *The 100 Best Companies to Work for in America.* New York: Plume, 1994.

Louv, Richard. *The Web of Life: Weaving the Values That Sustain Us.* Berkeley: Conari Press, 1996.

Maddox, Rebecca. *Your Dreams: For Any Woman Who Is Thinking about Her Own Business.* New York: Viking, 1995.

Morris, Betsy. "Is Your Family Wrecking Your Career?" *Fortune,* March 17, 1997: 70–73.

———. "Home-Office Heaven—and Hell." *Fortune,* March 17, 1997: 82–90.

Novak, Michael. *Business as a Calling: Work and the Examined Life.* New York: Free Press, 1996.

Olmstead, Barney. *The Job Sharing Handbook.* New York: Penguin Books, 1993.

Olson, Scott. *250 Home-Based Jobs: Innovative, Imaginative Alternatives to the World of 9 to 5!* New York: Prentice Hall, 1990.

O'Reilly, Brian. "The New Deal: What Companies and Employees Owe One Another." *Fortune,* June 13, 1994: 44–52.

Perspectives. "How Can Big Companies Keep the Entrepreneurial Spirit Alive?" *Harvard Business Review,* November–December 1995: 183–192.

Pilzar, Paul Zane. *God Wants You To Be Rich.* New York: Simon & Schuster, 1997.

Popcorn, Faith, and Lys Marigold. *Clicking: 16 Trends to Future Fit Your Life, Your Work, and Your Business.* New York: HarperCollins, 1996.

Pritchett, Price. *New Work Habits for a Radically Changing World.* Dallas: Pritchett & Associates, 1996.

Rice, Faye. "Champions of Communication." *Fortune,* June 3, 1991: 111–120.

Richman, Louis S. "How to Get Ahead in America." *Fortune,* May 16, 1994: 40–54.

Rifkin, Jeremy. *The End of Work: Technology, Jobs and Your Future: The Decline of the Global Labor Force and the Dawn of the Post-Market Era.* New York: G.P. Putnam's Sons, 1995.

Schechtman, Morris R. *Working without a Net: How to Survive and Thrive in Today's High Risk Business World.* New Jersey: Prentice Hall, 1994.

Schön, Donald A. *Educating the Reflective Practitioner: Toward a New Design for Teaching in the Professions.* San Francisco: Jossey-Bass, 1987.

Senge, Peter. *The Fifth Discipline: Mastering the Five Practices of the Learning Organization.* New York: Doubleday, 1990.

Serwer, Andrew. "America's 100 Fastest Growers." *Fortune,* August 9, 1993: 40–54.

Silver, A. David. *Quantum Companies: 100 Companies That Will Change the Face of Tomorrow's Business.* Princeton, N.J.: Peterson's/Pacesetter Books, 1995.

Smith, Lee. "Landing That First Real Job." *Fortune,* May 16, 1994: 58–60.

Stewart, Thomas A. "Brainpower." *Fortune,* June 3, 1991: 44–60.

———. "Get with the New Power Game." *Fortune,* January 13, 1997: 58–62.

———. "Planning a Career in a World without Managers." *Fortune,* March 20, 1995: 72–80.

———. "Your Company's Most Valuable Asset: Intellectual Capital." *Fortune,* October 3, 1994: 68–74.

"The Truth about Temping." *U.S. News & World Report,* November 1, 1993: 95.

Tully, Shawn. "The Modular Corporation." *Fortune,* February 8, 1993: 106.

———. "You'll Never Guess Who Really Makes . . ." *Fortune,* October 3, 1994: 124–128.

Vaill, Peter. *Learning As a Way of Being: Strategies for Survival in a World of Permanent White Water.* San Francisco: Jossey-Bass, 1996.

Valencia, Alis, ed. *At Work: Stories of Tomorrow's Workplace* (newsletter), March–April, 1995.

Warner, Melanie. "Working at Home: The Right Way to Be a Star in Your Bunny Slippers." *Fortune,* March 3, 1997: 165–166.

Wheatley, Margaret, and Myron Kellner-Rogers. *A Simpler Way.* San Francisco: Berrett-Koehler, 1996.

Yate, Martin. *Beat the Odds: Career Buoyancy Tactics for Today's Turbulent Job Market.* New York: Ballantine Books, 1995.

*I*ndex

About the Author

CAELA FARREN is committed to inspiring, advancing, and supporting mastery in the workplace. She is the CEO of MasteryWorks, Inc., an international human resources consulting and education firm. Current clients include Fortune 500 corporations, educational institutions, federal agencies, and small businesses looking for ways to increase intellectual capital. Her slogan, "Take a job and you'll work for a day; craft a profession and you'll work for life," is the basis of the work-systems theory in this book and the philosophy of her company.

For twenty-five years, Caela has pioneered paradigm shifts in the field of career development. Combining extensive research with practical applications, she has empowered individuals around the world to take charge of their careers. *Designing Career Development Systems*, which she coauthored, is considered a definitive work by human resources consultants. Hundreds of companies use this systems approach to career development to link individual career management to the changing needs of business. Caela is recognized internationally as a leading expert on career and workforce planning issues.

Caela holds a Ph.D. in organization development from Case Western Reserve University. She is a member of the Instructional Systems Association, the American Society for Training and Development, the O.D. Network, the World Future Society, and the Human Resource Planning Society. In 1996, Caela received the prestigious Walter Storey Career Development Professional Award from the American Society for Training and Development for outstanding contributions to career-management professionals. She lives with her daughter, Meaghan, in McLean, Virginia.

About MasteryWorks, Inc.

MasteryWorks, Inc., is the outcome of the merger of Career Systems, a pacesetter in career management publications, and Farren Associates, Inc., a nationally recognized human resources consulting firm. The company, based in Annandale, Virginia, specializes in designing educational tools, workshops, mentor-apprentice relationships, and experiences that assure work mastery at the personal, professional, and system levels.

Build Marketable and Meaningful Careers

- *Career Initiative Inventory™*—Are you clear about the 15 actions you can take to enhance your career? These simple actions can pay great dividends! (software version available)

- *TalentSort2000™ Cards*—Do you know how to choose jobs and projects that add value and are personally fulfilling? 52 cards show the way!

- *The Power of Networking™*—Networks are a key to success. Do you have the depth and breadth you need to handle the speed and complexity of ever-changing work demands? Only strong networks will allow you to *do more with less.*

- *Leading Career Indicators™*—Are you at risk due to changes in professions, industries, organizations, or jobs? By assessing the 40 indicators you can analyze your responses, assess potential risk(s) in each area, and gain a much clearer view of work and career vitality. (software version available)

- *Aligning Your Aspirations™*—Times are changing! Should you be expanding, exploring, or repackaging the way you work to feel more fulfilled and marketable?

- *Talent2000 Learning Plan™*—Can you make a business case for how your goals support organization strategies? Do you have a plan to back it up?

Assure Work and Life Balance

- *Awakening Purpose & Vision™*—Without a sense of purpose, life has little meaning! Do you have a clear and compelling mission and vision for your life?
- *LifeMastery Builder™*—Many people feel stressed or burned out! Do you have priorities and clear steps for managing the 12 basic needs of adult life? (software version available)
- *Living Your Values™*—Values change during a lifetime. Do you have a clear picture of what it takes to be in sync with your changing values?
- *The Twenty Year Journey™*—Do you know how you want to live in 5 to 10 years?—Are your dreams regarding health, work, family, economic security and home clear enough to show the actions you can take *now* to make those dreams a reality in the *future*?

Form and Join Smart Teams

- *TeamSmart™ Cards & Guide™*—Do you know your natural strengths when working with teams? Can you spot or correct a poorly performing team? *TeamSmart™* gives this kind of know-how in only minutes.

Caela and her colleagues have a thirty-five year track record of taking leading-edge theories in a variety of fields and integrating them into state-of-the-art learning tools. Their educational technology is codeveloped with masters in each profession and industry in which they consult. They have deep-seated belief that mastery comes from individual passion and years of guided practice with mentors.

For more information about MasteryWorks, Inc., products and services, please contact:

> MasteryWorks, Inc.
> 7353 McWhorter Place, Suite 200
> Annandale, VA 22003
> (800) 229-5712, fax (703) 256-9564
> http://www.masteryworks.com

For additional copies of

Who's Running Your Career?
Creating Stable Work
in Unstable Times

visit your local bookstore.

Or call MasteryWorks
(800) 229-5712
Fax (703) 256-9564
http://www.masteryworks.com

VISA / Mastercard / American Express
accepted

Quantity discounts are available.